Empowerment!

BECOME THE PERSON YOU WANT TO BE

MOSAICA PRESS

Empowerment!

BECOME THE PERSON YOU WANT TO BE

By Rabbi Sheea Langsam, LMHC, LPC

Foreword by Rabbi Shais Taub

Mosaica Press, Inc.

© 2016 by Mosaica Press

Designed and typeset by Daniella Kirsch

ISBN-10: 1-937887-86-3

ISBN-13: 978-1-937887-86-5

Published and distributed by:

Mosaica Press, Inc.
www.mosaicapress.com
info@mosaicapress.com

Rabbi Avrohom Spitzer
625 W. Kennedy Blvd.
Lakewood, N.J. 08701
(732) 961-9056

אברהם שפיצער
דומ"ץ
דקהל תולדות יעקב יוסף
דחסידי סקווירא – לעיקוואד

בס"ד

לפ"ק שנו

באתי בשורות אלו לברכת ידי"נ הנכבד שמח נאה אונ"ו יוסף
אלימלך שלום הי' אשר הראה לי פרי מעלליו אשר חבר בספר היקרת
בדרגל שבת והקדוש התורה וכולו כלו א' בדברי ספר הקדש
"אור החיים" אשר כיסף ואברהם שבחרו לתקשרו הקדוש צלאה
ולהביר מוק לעשוט, וכלל ישראל כולו ובראגהלת חסכם וכל
אאולם לנו נחלו בלשון צחבוי א' החיבור א' המקום באתי לברך ליבדיד
א' דאמר אלו אכרו לך כמה שלום לשיו ירו ורחק לא אצי
רות כו ובא הקבה ברורה ולשולה ובלוא אל שרבם
יהי, מעשה הלוי

הכו"ח בלב וותאי ברכות
אברהם שפיצר

TABLE OF CONTENTS

ACKNOWLEDGMENTS

The written word is a very poor and insufficient medium through which to express my appreciation and thanks to those who deserve it most. However, for lack of any better alternative, I will do my best.

"I will thank Hashem with my mouth and amongst multitudes I will praise him."[1] Before giving credit to the many wonderful people who have helped me, I have to give credit to Whom it is really due. It is only with Hashem's great help that I have reached this great milestone of publishing my first book. It was He Who first planted the ideas in my head and then helped me formulate those vague ideas into palatable articles. Hashem then led me step-by-step through the entire process.

In fact, Hashem started working on this book long before I did. It started the moment I was born. My ideas and thought process is in great part a result of the great family into which Hashem has placed me. I was extremely lucky to know three of my grandparents, and each

---

1   *Tehillim* 109:30.

one influenced me in a unique way. My grandparents had all witnessed the horrors of the Holocaust; they had lost their near and dear but they didn't suffer from "survivor's syndrome." They were all full of joie de vivre. I learned from them that one need not stay stuck in a problem. It's possible to see the light even through very dark tunnels.

My grandmother, Mrs. Faige Langsam *yblch"t*, is a self-proclaimed billionaire by merit of all the good Hashem has bestowed upon her. One would never guess that this upbeat woman experienced more than her fair share of misfortunes. She continues to inspire me with her exceptionally positive outlook. She is also my link to a world where the self is no more than a vessel to help others.

I would like to express my sincerest appreciation to my dear parents who have directly and indirectly influenced the creation of this book. My father has been a true role model. He is truly exceptional in that his ego was never a factor in his life, and he thus possesses a rare clarity of view. While I have, unfortunately, not inherited this quality, it provided me a peek into a world free of ego-imposed obstructions.

My mother is a fount of intuitive wisdom. Not only does she possess an astounding breadth of knowledge in standard psychology, she has an inexhaustible trove of novel approaches to ease the complications that crop up in life. Whenever I found myself stuck while writing this book, she had a solution ready.

My father sees no complications and my mother has a remedy for every complication. I have neither of these traits, but I have picked up some things between the two of them.

My deepest appreciation goes to my dear in-laws who helped me in every way possible to bring this book to fruition. They were always there to cheer me on, from my schooling to establishing my practice, and on to my publishing this book. They have been my inspiration in the way they so selflessly devote themselves to the community and to individuals in an unpretentious way. Even more importantly, they gave me my wife who has stood by my side and supported me in all my endeavors. She gave me the confidence to follow my dreams and to persevere even when the road was bumpy.

Many thanks to my dear friend and neighbor, Rabbi Moshe Yehuda Blum. Despite his demanding schedule as a sought-after *mechanech*, he spent numerous hours reviewing the content of this book and delving into the minutiae in order to ensure that it is fully compatible with the Torah view.

I owe a tremendous debt of gratitude to my dear aunt and uncle, Rabbi Shlomo and Mindy Torn. In an unassuming way, they go to great lengths to help others. Their exceptional readiness to help me in any and every way made this book a reality.

Rabbi Shais Taub has become a household name and a role model for the seamless fusion of timeless Torah wisdom and psychology. His profound insight and keen understanding of the human psyche are astounding. He has raised the prestige of emotional health practitioners among the *frum* population. I am honored that he agreed to write the foreword for this book.

I feel honored to have been able to work with the wonderful staff at Mosaica Press. Our relationship was more than a regular working relationship. They took this personally. They saw potential in my original manuscript and they guided me through the process of turning a good manuscript into a great book. I couldn't have done it without them.

FOREWORD

Torah is wisdom, as in "Your wisdom and understanding in the eyes of the nations."[2] However, there are different kinds of wisdom. Some wisdom is philosophical while some wisdom is practical. It should never be forgotten that as much as the truths of Torah are ultimately beyond human understanding, Torah is also a practical guide for everyday life. As the *Zohar* explains, the very word Torah comes from the word *hora'ah*, literally direction or instruction.[3]

If I may editorialize, I believe it is this aspect of Torah — its eminently practical side — that is often overlooked even by those who revere Torah for its wisdom. Unfortunately, in our generation there is a tendency even among Torah observant individuals to search in foreign pastures for guidance in life under the banner of "If they tell you there

---

2   *Devarim* 4:6.
3   *Zohar III* 53b.

is wisdom among the nations, believe them."[4] Of course, they don't quote the rest of the sentence, "If they tell you there is Torah among the nations, don't believe them."

Torah is *Toras Chaim* and *Toras Emes*. That is to say that Torah's truth is not just a philosophical truth, but also a practical truth that works in everyday living.

I have read passages from this book by Rabbi Sheea Langsam and have been duly impressed by the author's dedication to highlighting a genuine Torah approach to many of the questions asked by people today. In down-to-earth and simple language, the author makes it clear how Torah and its commentaries (particularly the Ohr HaChaim HaKadosh) provide clear guidance for many of the issues that perplex today's generation.

The simplicity and accessibility of the author's style not only facilitates the easy understanding of concepts but will also put readers at ease, I am sure, with its unassuming style. One of the greatest obstacles to personal growth is the ego. The student must do all he or she can to be humble, but by the same token, teachers must do all they can to not purposely threaten the students' egos. Torah teachers who intimidate their students — whether intellectually, by purposely speaking above their understanding, or morally, by condemning them — elicit unnecessary resistance. Especially in today's world when so many people earnestly seek clarity, a lighter touch is ultimately more powerful than a stern hand, and in this respect the author has succeeded.

Ultimately, the greatest compliment one can pay a Torah thinker is by saying that they have truly said nothing new. The author's insights in this book, while presented in an original and creative manner, are not new at all. So while the book contains a plethora of contemporary anecdotes, references, and scenarios that will put the modern era at ease, the basic ideas being expressed are timeless. I was particularly pleased to see that footnotes were used to clearly indicate Torah sources.

In our day and age, when the darkness of exile is so palpable, an even greater light is needed, and this light — the light of Torah — is also

---

4   *Midrash, Eichah Rabbah* 17.

the glimmer of the coming dawn of Redemption, of which the Rambam writes in the conclusion of his Mishnah Torah:

"In that era, there will be neither famine nor war, envy nor competition, for good will flow in abundance, and all the delights will be freely available as dust. The occupation of the entire world will be solely to know G-d. Therefore, the Jews will be great sages and know the hidden matters, grasping the knowledge of their Creator according to the full extent of human potential, as it states, 'The world will be filled with the knowledge of G-d as the waters cover the ocean bed.'"[5]

In other words, not only is the light of Torah desperately needed in these final days of exile, but even more so, by revealing the light of Torah we are actually experiencing a foretaste of what is to come in the era of redemption, may it be immediately.

Rabbi Shais Taub
Pittsburgh, PA

---

5   *Yeshayahu* 11:9.

INTRODUCTION

Dave was lost in the forest. The day had started uneventfully. What was supposed to be a standard hike ended up being anything but. He had even taken along a map of the trails just in case, but it was of little help. He simply didn't know how to read the map. Dave felt lost and alone. The trees all looked alike to him and no matter how many times he tried finding his way out, he just ended up back on the same spot having walked in circles. There was no one in sight and he was terrified of having to spend the night in the forest.

Suddenly, to Dave's great relief, another hiker came along. This person showed him how to read the map and which markers to look out for. The hiker moved on, but for Dave this little bit of help made all the difference. He now knew what to look for and how to follow the trail. Before long he found himself out of the forest.

Hashem has placed us in the forest of life. He provided us with a map to help us safely navigate our way through the forest. We were each granted the tools and the ability to succeed in life and to maximize our potential. The problem arises when we forget how to read the map. This could happen for a variety of reasons. Our egos could be obstructing our vision. Self-doubt could cause us to question our abilities. At times, the influences from our surroundings could distract us from focusing on our map.

When these things happen, we start feeling a little lost and we can experience a sense of dissatisfaction. We might start feeling unhappy in certain areas of our life. We suddenly want things to be different. At times, we're not even sure exactly what it is that's bothering us, but there is this niggling feeling that's just refusing to let go. It's at such times that we could benefit from someone coming around and helping us read the map.

This book was designed to do just that.

BOOK PURPOSE

The purpose of this book is to serve as an eye-opener and to help us identify possible faulty reasoning and behaviors that have been hampering our ability to move forward. I named the book EMPOWERMENT because once these obstructions are removed we will naturally feel empowered to make the changes necessary. We'll be able to tap into our inner resources and bring out the best in ourselves.

This book is not a self-help book and was not designed to help treat serious disorders. For that, much more comprehensive work is needed, often with the assistance of a professional. This book was written to offer inspiration and to provide a gentle nudge for us to take a second look at our lives.

The book provides us with a sort of outsider's look — outside our egos — on our lives. This vantage point could help us take note of possible obstructions and/or the humorous circles we might be walking in. This would hopefully set us thinking in the right direction. Just thinking in the right direction alone is half the salvation. The book will also guide us towards the other half, which calls for some soul-searching and reaching into ourselves. At times, I also provide some practical tips to make otherwise vague concepts more practical for actual use. We will then be in a much better position to bring out the best in us and to maximize our potential.

BOOK STRUCTURE

The book is divided into four sections, representing four major areas of our lives. They are: Self, Interpersonal, Marriage, and *Chinuch*.

Self — There is no one we spend more time with than ourselves. We could be our best friend and greatest enemy simultaneously. While this would be totally absurd if it were anyone else, with ourselves we're fine with it. We wake up with this reality and we go to sleep with this reality and we might not even give it too much thought. It could, however, create an uncomfortable feeling within us where we could almost hear two opposing voices in our heads. This could create within us the uncomfortable feeling known as cognitive dissonance.

Interpersonal — So much of our life revolves around our interactions with others. Social life is a two-sided coin. On the obverse, our interactions with others could serve as a source of fulfillment and joy. It could provide us with many opportunities to bring out the best in us. It could also help boost our confidence. On the reverse, it could also agitate some weaker parts of our personality. Social life could be a major source of self-doubt and anxiety.

Marriage — You can't live with it, you can't live without it. It's a high-stakes game. There's nothing that could provide a feeling of stability, a sense of belonging, a feeling of being loved, needed, fulfilled, and appreciated as marriage. On the other hand, a marriage gone sour could inflict more emotional damage on a person than just about anything.

Chinuch — Children provide us with a whole new set of opportunities and challenges. Child rearing affords us a sense of purpose. We can impart in our children a love for Hashem and His Torah and mitzvos. Along with that, we can pass on our family legacy, the traditions and the wisdom we have worked hard to attain over the years. *Chinuch* is bursting with opportunities. However, while children are part of us, they are also individuals. This could sometimes cause us to get frustrated when our children act differently than we hoped for.

The book contains a total of fifty chapters. In each chapter we'll explore one specific area within those four categories where we might have become stuck.

The very nature of writing about areas we might have become stuck in dictates that I mention some of our shortcomings. In no way does this imply that we are flawed people and full of problems. To the contrary, anyone reading this book is obviously on a quest to improve, and there is nothing more positive and encouraging than that!

To make the ride more enjoyable, I started off each chapter with a vignette. These include echoes of history. As hindsight is always twenty-twenty, looking back on history could afford us an amazing perspective. There are also reflections on current events. Looking at the issues from the broad lens of current events can offer us a unique viewpoint. At other times I used true life stories, as there is nothing that can drive a point home as well as a good story. To protect the confidentiality of the subjects, all identifying details have been changed. While some stories may seem somewhat overdone to the uninitiated, those who have experienced similar situations will readily be able to identify with the characters in the story.

The vignettes are followed with an insight from the Ohr HaChaim relevant to the discussion. This is something personal and close to my heart. For a number of years now, I've been learning the wonderful *peirush* of the Ohr HaChaim on the Torah. The more I delved into the timeless wisdom of his words, the more I realized that embedded within his explanation on the Torah are numerous priceless insights to help decode the human mystery. Many perplexities that have plagued mankind for millennia are succinctly explained in a few short words. Coming from a background of psychology, I was amazed to find the basis of many new psychological theories already outlined by the Ohr HaChaim. The Ohr HaChaim offers unparalleled depth along with a clear Torah perspective.

The contents of this book first appeared in a weekly column in some magazines. The positive feedback from the articles was overwhelming, and it served as the impetus for printing it in book form. I invested great effort in presenting the ideas in simple layman's terms in order to make it enjoyable to read and easy to grasp. Fasten your seatbelts as we set out on this amazingly empowering discovery trip. We'll explore the foibles and fickleness of mankind. Along the way, we'll learn some amazing survival tips to help us survive and thrive in the wilderness of life.

Enjoy!

SELF-EMPOWERMENT

WAKE UP THE
SLEEPING GIANT

T hey sat around in shul and discussed the pressing
matter at hand. It was obvious that things couldn't
stay this way. There were suggestions flying back
and forth as the short break between Minchah and
Maariv flew by. Everyone was in agreement that "someone"
had to do "something" because "things" had to change. With
the start of Maariv, the impromptu meeting came to a close
while the topic remained open. This scene would repeat itself
almost on a daily basis.

The ladies on the block also weighed in on the matter at every
occasion. They too came to the conclusion that the "situation" had to change and "someone" had to do "something"
about it. Amazingly, for a change, the men and women were
of the same opinion.

Puzzlingly, despite all the serious discussions, nothing changed. Everybody just looked on in exasperation as the "situation" kept on deteriorating. Everyone had many justifiable reasons why they simply weren't suited for the job, why they couldn't be the ones to take charge. Everyone was waiting for that born-and-bred *askan* to step up and take charge. But, alas, the community boasted no graduates from The School of *Askanus*.

After all was said and done, a lot was said and absolutely nothing was done!

Then, R' Yaakov had enough and he decided to actually do something. He'd never been an *askan* and he had no intention of becoming one. He simply came to the realization that he bore equal responsibility with everyone else. It wasn't easy at first for R' Yaakov to go public, and he did it very reluctantly. However, as he became more involved in *klal* work, he discovered that he'd greatly underestimated his capabilities. There was so much more to him than he'd dared imagine. It would have been a shame had he not afforded himself the opportunity to tap into all those hidden resources.

TORAH LESSON

The Torah uses two metaphors for Torah study: "Like a downpour on the vegetation and like raindrops on the blades of grass."[6] The Torah juxtaposes mature and solid vegetation with a downpour and the fragile blades of grass with droplets of rain. The Ohr HaChaim explains that this is to teach us that we each need to maximize our capabilities. Those who are like solid vegetation need to take on elevated levels of Torah study like the full force of a rainstorm. We ought not feel so accomplished when we extend ourselves a little bit. Our accomplishments need to be measured in comparison to our capabilities.

---

6   *Devarim* 32:2.

On the day of reckoning, we'll be held accountable for all the latent capabilities that we failed to tap into. Those with greater capabilities will be called to task even for not delving into the secrets of the Celestial Chariot. There is no room for complacency. Good enough is not good enough!

LIFE LESSON

Who enjoys lazing around?

While we may have never been exposed to laziness, chances are that we are familiar with its relative — complacency. How good and how soothing complacency feels! It allows us to snuggle up and feel comfortable wherever we are without any unnecessary pressure to take initiative. No need to overextend ourselves and venture into unchartered territory. We don't have to risk becoming too pressured by taking more commitments upon ourselves. We can just leave things the way they are. How practical!

Truth be told, we sometimes do have a fleeting thought to shake ourselves out of our immobilizing complacency. But we quickly drown those maverick thoughts in a sea of justifications and excuses.

Honestly, taking initiative can appear challenging. We might not believe that we possess the necessary qualifications for the job. We possibly fear the reactions of others. Above all there is the fear of the unknown. We just don't know how our lives will change by taking on something new. Staying grounded affords us the comforting feeling of standing on terra firma; there is no falling from there. However, we're really doing ourselves a terrible disservice. There is so much potential within us just waiting to burst forth. Through complacency, the greater part of our capabilities may remain latent forever. We could be missing the very reason that Hashem created us! What a shame!

Yes, it is surely disconcerting and unsettling, but true nonetheless. Some of us really are functioning at the lower end of our capabilities. We are willingly settling for less without any justifiable excuses. Why? Why should we not be fair to ourselves and allow ourselves the opportunity to make use of our wealth of innate resources? Why should we be guilty of the crime of robbing ourselves of our true value? How comfortable can we be with ourselves when we know that we've become addicted to the numbing and dumbing drug known as complacency? Let us think about it. Are we truly ready to jeopardize so much of our personality and potential just for the short-lived pleasure that this drug offers?

Now, let us picture how much more meaningful and fulfilled our lives could be. How much more alive could we be if we allowed more of our being to actually live! Let us discover our vast capabilities, and let's tap into them. Let's wake up the sleeping giant within us!

Let us each have a look at the many things — big or small — that we've been waiting for an elusive someone to come and take charge of. We should pick one area where we will take the leap of faith and have trust in our own capabilities and make it our project. The more we apply ourselves to our new undertaking, the more we'll notice how our personalities stretch, the more of ourselves we'll use, and the fuller our lives will be! Why should we shortchange ourselves? We owe it to ourselves to live our life to its fullest!

When we'll live to our fullest, we'll feel much more fulfilled!

LET'S PLAY THE BEST GAME

R' Dovid felt that he was a failure. Period. He knew that he didn't even stand a chance in the game of life. His parents had never given him confidence. They had never taught him how to think on his own. They had never afforded him any opportunities to take charge. He was already marrying off kids and R' Dovid was still entangled and stuck in his past.

R' Dovid's present existence was one of misery and dysfunction, all because of his childhood experiences with his parents. He couldn't hold down a job because his parents had told him he'd never be able to stay put for too long. He didn't have friends because his mother had always told him that he was a loner. He couldn't stand up to his *mechutanim* because his father always admonished him that he had no backbone.

The way R' Dovid saw it there was no way to undo the damaging programming of his parents. His only hope was in his next *gilgul* — if he'd be born to better parents.

At times, when R' Dovid felt overwhelmed by his helplessness, he'd burst out in a fit of anger at what his parents had done to him. He would then remember that his father always had similar outbursts and realize that he, Dovid, surely inherited that tendency from his father. He then got mad at his father for never having worked on his anger issue, thus causing Dovid to take after him. Whenever something would go wrong, R' Dovid would instantly find something and someone to blame it on, primarily his parents.

TORAH LESSON

After the *mabul* Hashem promised to never again curse the earth, "For the inclination of the heart of man is evil from his youth."[7] The Ohr HaChaim compares it to a bull that has been trained to fight, which the Gemara says is *patur* when it gores because it was trained to do just that.[8] So too, man ought not to be held accountable for his actions, as the evil inclination preceded his birth. For any wrong we do we can blame our inborn evil inclination. We're not at fault; we've been preprogrammed to desire evil!

However, the Ohr HaChaim says, convincing as it may sound, blaming won't get us anywhere! As humans, we are imbued with the ability to overcome our early programming as well as any other obstacle that may come our way. Early conditioning and obstacles we've encountered may afford us some leeway, but by-and-large we are the only ones responsible for our actions. Blaming is for the bulls; we humans are above that!

---

7   *Bereishis* 8:21.
8   *Bava Kama* 39a.

LIFE LESSON

Who ever said that chess was the most creative and brilliant game ever created?

Sure, chess is a brilliant game, and no two games are alike no matter how often it is played, but the one game that is even greater and can be played for many years continuously is the blame game!

It is undoubtedly one of the best and most imaginative games ever to have been invented! It is played by all ages and has been translated into every language. The rules sound pretty simple and easy to follow, but, in reality, it is very complex and played differently every time. From the bored international diplomats who play it in the hallowed halls of the UN down to the little kids who play it in the school yard, everyone seems to enjoy it! There have been recorded instances of the game being played continuously for generations! Nations are known to play it against each other. Everyone is fond of it!

Widespread as this game may be, the best at playing it are, arguably, kids who play it against their parents. We have in recent years become so enamored of this form of the blame game that we've started accepting it as the truth! Intelligent as we believe we are, we feel comfortable blaming our personal ills on our parents. We've duped ourselves into believing that a person is a helpless product of early conditioning. We have willingly exchanged the powerful force of free will for the short-lived thrill of the blame game. How gullible we are!

While there is no question that the impact parents have on their children is powerful and all encompassing, this cannot excuse wrongful adult behavior.

Why should we live all our adult years in the shadow of what transpired when we were young? Are we adults meant to be lifelong prisoners at the mercy of our inner child? The mere thought of this should make us discard the blame game with a vengeance! And we can do it!

(There are some schools of modern psychology that do encourage the notion that many — if not most — of our emotional and behavioral shortcomings are the direct results of early childhood traumas. Even if we ascribe to this school of thought, we still have the free will — and the ability — to go ahead and fix up whatever needs fixing.)

Unless we enjoy feeling like programmed animals, we might do well to remember that, as humans, we are not bound to the shackles of our youth. Just like we graduated to larger shoes and larger desks, we should also graduate to a larger frame of mind. We possess within ourselves the power to override early impressions.

Let's remember that, like every game, the blame game, exciting as it may be, has no bearing on reality. Placing the blame on someone else will in no way make the problem disappear. The situation will remain exactly the same and we will continue to suffer as even more opportunities of blame-placing arise. However, if we decide to graduate blame school we stand a chance of actually moving ahead in life. The very thought should be exciting and invigorating.

When we find ourselves consciously or subconsciously blaming our parents for something, let's make a conscious decision to break free of these shackles. Let's remember that as adults we have the ability to take the reins of our lives into our own hands. Instead of wasting our adult years by constantly reliving those few childhood years, let's enjoy living as productive adults!

There are no winners in the blame game —
only losers!

BECOME YOUR OWN BOSS!

P u Yi was the last emperor of China. As a Buddhist emperor, he was also worshiped as a deity. Pu Yi was crowned at the tender age of two and was forcefully removed from his parents' home and taken to the formidable palace complex, popularly known as the Forbidden City.

Pu Yi became completely cut off from normal human life. He had absolutely no contact with the outside world and he had no idea what it meant to be a kid. Any regular, age-appropriate misbehavior from Pu Yi would send his ministers into a panic. They were convinced that anytime their god diverged from the rigid protocol it would impact the heavenly constellations and the earthly politics. The ministers were at a loss; allowing the emperor to behave as he pleased endangered the very existence of the world, but punishing and spanking the deity was equally perilous and unthinkable! So a great and practical solution was found: any time Pu Yi misbehaved, a designated servant took the beating.

This arrangement spared the heavens and earth from destruction, but it set Pu Yi up for self-destruction. He grew up to be an extremely egocentric, inconsiderate, and insatiable individual. When he was dethroned by revolutionaries at the ripe old age of fifteen, the former deity had no skills and no idea how to function as a member of society. Pu Yi got away with spankings as a devilish little deity, but his not having attained the skill of accountability haunted him all his life.

TORAH LESSON

We were brought up with the concept that an inadvertent sin, a *shogeig*, is more easily forgiven; in the times of the Beis Hamikdash, the unintentional sinner brought a *korban* and was forgiven. In civil law, however, once a misdeed is done, one is held accountable whether the act was intentional or not. Chazal tell us[9] that when it was asked through *nevuah* what the sentence for the unintentional sinner should be, there was a proclamation made: "The soul that sins shall die!"[10] How then can the slaughtering of an animal compensate for the misdeeds of a person? (Never mind what PETA would have to say about it!) How could a *korban* rectify a sin *b'shogeig*?

The Ohr HaChaim[11] explains it with a Chazal, which states that a person does not sin unless he (temporarily) loses his senses.[12] In other words, he becomes like an animal, incapable of mature thought. When he comes to his senses and repents, he regains his status as a man. Since the Torah does not wish to hold a man responsible for actions he did

---

9   Talmud Yerushalmi, *Makkos* 2:6.
10   *Yechezkel* 18:4.
11   *Vayikra* 9:8.
12   *Zohar I*, 121a.

while in an animal state, the sinner is commanded to bring a *korban* and watch as the animal is slaughtered, feeling its pain and realizing the animal has taken his place. This will help him atone for the sin he committed in his animalistic state.

Thus, Hashem's commandments are fair and just, as this is the most balanced form of accountability.

LIFE LESSON

What is the greatest invention ever devised?

Excuses!

Maybe it's not the greatest, but it surely features prominently on the list of great inventions. Excuses are so powerful and profound! There is nothing quite like a good excuse to help one avoid accountability and still feel comfortable about it.

Excuses have been around for some time now; in fact, since the times of Cain they have existed. We have collectively invested a lot of time and effort in perfecting the art of excuses while accountability has been relegated to the naïve.

Our excuses are so good that we don't only give them to others but even to ourselves! We regularly concoct excuses to cover up our own shortcomings. What's more is that we are actually the primary recipients for our own excuses. Whenever we are beset by guilt or frustration over a true or perceived shortcoming, we instantly fabricate an excuse to soothe our conscience. We then enthusiastically embrace and believe our self-fabricated excuses. How creative! How incredible!

Even when we do occasionally shake ourselves free of our gullibility, we still find it difficult to let go of the excuse modality. It serves the great purpose of allowing us to avoid confronting our inadequacies. It allows us to continue pretending that all is fine and dandy. But, alas, we really are too smart to continually let ourselves be fooled by our own excuses. When we get fed up with hearing them, we start to beat ourselves up and feel like losers, so all we end up gaining from our excuses are lost opportunities!

Let us stop excusing ourselves as victims of circumstance. Let us take ownership of our lives and our shortcomings. True, ownership comes with responsibility, but it is well worth it. Ownership will provide us with many privileges that are only available to members of the executive club, such as:

- The ability to change things we don't like.
- The ability to set goals and obtain them.
- The liberating and empowering feeling of being in control of our lives.

Now that we have voted ourselves in as CEOs of our lives, we carry executive responsibilities and must tackle the things that have been bothering us. We are in the position to take an objective look at ourselves and set real goals. As our own bosses we are accountable to no one but ourselves, and that is the toughest part! We can't allow ourselves to accept excuses that don't make sense. Instead of wasting our resources on concocting creative excuses, we should utilize these same resources to come up with innovative ways to solve our problems and thus make our enterprises flourish!

CAUTION: DON'T OVERDO IT!

Too much accountability isn't good, either. It could cause us to fall into the trap of blaming ourselves even for things that are truly beyond our control. Why should we be so unfair to ourselves? It serves no purpose other than allowing ourselves to be consumed by misplaced guilt. Misplaced guilt can, in turn, create a lot of extra baggage, and why should we claim ownership of baggage that is not our own?

Winners have no need for excuses.

CAUTION: HONORABLE TRAP AHEAD!

The Saudi prince is fabulously wealthy. He owns sizeable shares in many successful companies and has taken extravagance to a whole new level. His indulgences include sprawling palace complexes, an exhaustive collection of luxury vehicles — including a jewel encrusted Mercedes, a massive yacht, and a private jumbo jet with a throne room. Anything that can be imagined and created he undertakes to obtain.

One would think that all his pricey "toys" affords the prince some peace and contentment, but that is not the case. The prince craves honor and recognition like an addict and will go to any lengths to guarantee a continuous flow of positive reports in the news, with his public relations department working overtime to mold and create a fascinating image of him. When journalists indicate an interest in the prince, they receive an amazing portfolio with doctored magazines that extol the virtues of the prince.

More than anything, the prince is hooked on the annual Forbes list. His holdings always show a temporary rise in his gains over the ten weeks preceding the publication of the list. Honor is his end goal, and he'll use every means to accomplish his goal.

TORAH LESSON

The Torah relates that Pharaoh searched for ways to outwit Bnei Yisrael and ensnare them into bondage in Egypt. [13] Pharaoh appointed tax officials over them, with taxes meaning physical labor required of Bnei Yisrael for the state. The Ohr HaChaim is bothered by the lack of any wit or ruse on Pharaoh's part to devise this plan. Additionally, he asks, how did Bnei Yisrael fall for it and allow themselves to be drafted into slave labor?

The Ohr HaChaim explains that Pharaoh didn't place upon them officials of taxes; rather, he assigned this honorable title on Jews themselves. These officials were to oversee the efficiency of the kingdom's labor tax. The ruse was offering Bnei Yisrael these positions of "honor," and they fell for it. This made it easy for the Egyptian authorities, who made sure that there was a perpetual shortage of tax laborers. The Jewish tax officials then felt compelled to lend a hand in order to get the work completed on schedule. When there was an extreme shortage of laborers they asked their relatives to chip in, and it wasn't long before Bnei Yisrael was fully enslaved.

LIFE LESSON

What's the most addictive substance in the world?
Honor, of course!

---

13   *Shemos* 1:11.

Many millions of people are addicted to honor and the government hasn't banned it! In fact, Washington DC has one of the most active markets for the honor substance. Many great Washingtonian politicians rely on the honor drug to give them a high and to stimulate their productivity. The honor production industry the world over is booming, as people and governments waste billions of dollars annually to satisfy this addiction. The honor market offers an enormous variety of products to satisfy every taste and budget.

It's incredible to think of the amount of honor that has been used over thousands of years, and yet the supply hasn't run dry. It is still being mined in great quantities and new production lines are added all the time. Even more absurd is that no matter how much honor is produced, it always seems to be in short supply. The demand is far greater than the supply.

The honor drug is so potent that it affects our neural system almost instantly. As soon as we imbibe it, our prefrontal cortex is rendered useless, and our judgment becomes marred. We easily become hooked on honor and we crave it to distraction; we'd do almost anything to receive another dose. This leaves us at risk of being exploited by those in the position to provide us with additional doses of the drug, much like with any other substance addiction. It's unbelievable how much we're ready to pay for something so totally worthless!

Unfortunately, as of yet, no Honor-Seekers Anonymous program has been established for honor addicts so we have no choice but to work on it ourselves. Whenever we begin to feel a craving for an honor boost, let us remind ourselves that by imbibing honor we are willingly surrendering control of our lives. Not a very good idea!

However, in no way does this mean that we have to forgo the sweet taste of honor and recognition completely. In fact, our need for recognition is part of our very makeup. We could, and should, indulge in generous doses of this mind-altering delicacy, but we need not pay for it. We can get it free of charge and without compromising on our free will and self-control by producing it ourselves.

We can start out by honoring ourselves and reminding ourselves how good and special we are. We should look out for commendable acts that we have done and give ourselves credit and recognition for those actions. While it might feel awkward at first, we will get used to it with some practice and begin to appreciate it. In all probability it will not completely do away with our desire for outside recognition and honor, but it will definitely curb it to a great extent. We'll cease walking around in a daze, desperately searching for every crumb of recognition, but we'll still have the option of indulging in it on occasion.

Once we've practiced this home-brewed honor formula on ourselves, we can start distributing some of it to our loved ones and acquaintances and make them feel special and appreciated. We can find their strong points and offer recognition for those strengths. Even at no charge we'll gain immensely from honoring others, because they'll usually reciprocate and not charge us for the service either. Even better, we'll create an environment of positivity and a drive to do better; everyone would thrive in such an environment.

So, there really is no need for Honor-Seekers Anonymous. In fact, there is no reason be anonymous. Let's be very vocal in our doling out of honors!

Let's not disgrace ourselves by seeking honor
from others.

DON'T WANT IT — HAVE IT!

Mordy was a success story. He worked hard, allowing himself little time for anything other than work, but it paid off. His investments were highly profitable and his business interests continuously increased. Mordy's name occasionally graced the papers and his presence enhanced many organizations' board of directors. Mordy housed his family in a fine edifice that would do many a French nobleman proud.

Mordy had every apparent reason to be happy. However, it seemed that no matter how swiftly he climbed the socio-economic ladder, he was always one step behind happiness. Contentment dangled teasingly just beyond Mordy's reach. He couldn't locate it on his exotic vacations or in his stately boardrooms, nor was it included in bank statements.

However, Mordy was not one to be easily dissuaded. His many disappointments notwithstanding, he never gave up his search for happiness. He became ever more creative in the venues and locations that he'd search for it, but alas, happiness remained one step ahead of him.

TORAH LESSON

After seven years of plenty, a devastating hunger struck Egypt. Yosef immediately opened all the granaries and started selling food. Why did Yosef open all the storehouses at once? Wouldn't it have been wiser to sell from one granary at a time, and only when one location was empty to move on to the next?

The Ohr HaChaim explains that it was part of Yosef's strategy to keep the citizens' hunger at bay.[14] Yosef understood the nature of mankind and he knew that satiation is as much the work of the mind as of the stomach. If there would be a perception of lack, it would increase the want. People would crave food much more and feel much hungrier if they felt there was not enough to be had. He therefore opened all the warehouses at once so the people would see there was no lack of food.

LIFE LESSON

We're all satisfied with our lots, are we not?

We may desire a lot of things, but that doesn't necessarily mean we're not happy with what we already have — we just want more. And while we're taught from an early age to be happy with our lot, it's possible that we never fully internalized this lesson since we still feel that acquiring more would bring us greater happiness. We believe that would our goods to multiply, our happiness would expand in tandem. This thought process makes sense, doesn't it?

Truth be told, it does make a lot of sense, otherwise there wouldn't be so many sensible people thinking along these lines.

---

14   *Bereishis* 41:56.

So what's wrong with this way of thinking? Since we prefer not to feel miserable as we try endlessly to fill the bottomless pit known as "a lot," it would be worthwhile to take a closer look at ourselves.

When we set out on the journey to acquire lots of goods and happiness, we have to pack up enough reserves of happiness. The journey to happiness via acquisitions tends to be a taxing one, and we easily become miserable and disillusioned in our quest.

So before heading out, let's allow ourselves a moment to reflect. When we want something, we in essence believe that we lack that thing. And so long as that lack isn't filled, we'll feel like something is missing, holding us back from feeling a sense of completeness. Mr. Noah Webster, while not necessarily a psychologist, was quite proficient in the English language. In his book, Webster's Dictionary, he writes "lack" as a definition for "want."

Our minds are simply amazing: We could possess so much good and feel content, yet as soon as we want something new to increase our happiness, our minds let us believe that we are actually lacking that thing. As we all know, lack and contentment are uncomfortable in each other's presence. Hence, as soon as we convince ourselves that we really lack something, we start to feel unhappy. We actually subject ourselves to the pain and suffering of unhappiness for the goal of being even happier. How absurd!

So rather than embark on this perilous journey to fill the gaping holes created by our wants and lacks, let us find an easier way to attain happiness. By outsmarting ourselves and fooling our minds into producing more happiness hormones, we can acquire this elusive commodity called true happiness.

It's not quite as complicated as it sounds. First, let's examine the workings of our minds. The primary tool in the mind's arsenal is the thinking process. When we spy an enticing product our minds go into overdrive, flooding us with thoughts of how great life could be if only we'd acquire that item. With enough such thoughts filling our minds we actually start believing them, and, soon enough, we buy into the nonsense. Before we know it, we've been convinced that happiness is impossible unless we've filled our desires.

Becoming aware of the modus operandi of our brains will allow us to not fall prey to these thoughts. Ironically, we can use this very same tool of our minds to the opposite effect. If we make it a habit to spend a few minutes a day focusing on all the good we already have, we can flood our minds with positive thoughts of how good it is to have all this good. Let's think about it some more. These positive thoughts will start pushing themselves to the forefront of our minds, and we'll start feeling content with the things we already have. Once we lay claim to this feeling of happiness for a large portion of the day, we can finally risk embarking on the draining journey of acquiring additional things with happiness as our goal. Up until this point, it would have been too risky to try to obtain more happiness, since we'd spend our time and money only to find that our happiness could not be bought.

Happiness can be ours free of charge — there's no need to waste money on it!

MAXIMIZING LEISURE

f one were to look for a vacation that would miss the point, then the picturesque village of Chelm would surely be the destination of choice. Chelm's very culture was based on missing the point and engaging in pointless activities.

One day, the *rav* set out to catch the train to a neighboring town where he was invited to speak. Once at the station, the *rav* suddenly realized that he was missing his notes. The *rav* informed his companions of his predicament, stating that he believed he'd left the notes on his desk. The quickest runner from among his disciples was hastily dispatched to return to the *rav*'s house and check his desk for the precious notes.

The train arrived in the interim, but the *rav*'s devoted followers begged the conductor to hold up the train. They were worried about their *rav*'s ability to deliver his speech without his notes. Should the *rav* stumble it would reflect poorly on their prestigious *kehillah*.

After a few tense minutes, the panting *bachur* returned —
without the notes. He happily informed the anxious crowd
that the *rav* was indeed right — the notes had been on his
desk. The crowd was delighted at this confirmation of their
great *rav*'s memory. The *rav* boarded the train without his
notes, content with the knowledge that he had accurately
remembered where he'd left them.

TORAH LESSON

The Torah enumerates the travels and travails of Bnei Yisrael in the *mid-bar*. The Ohr HaChaim asks, Why does the Torah place the emphasis on the
masa'os, the travels, and not on the *chanayos*, the encampments?[15] Instead of
starting the *perek* with, "These are the wanderings of Bnei Yisrael," the Torah
should have started out, "These are the encampments of Bnei Yisrael." After
all, the travels were merely a means to get to the various resting destinations!

The Ohr HaChaim explains: The travels through the wilderness
served a very lofty purpose. There were holy sparks that were held in
captivity in the wilderness, the habitat of the forces of evil. Hashem
sent Bnei Yisrael to those very places where the sparks were in captivity
to free them and gain possession of those precious sparks.

Never before did the Bnei Yisrael experience such an intense con-
centration of *kedushah* — the confluence of the *kedushah* of *am Yisrael*
in its entirety, the Torah, and the holiness of Moshe and Aharon. They
were therefore able to overpower the forces of evil that ensnared those
precious sparks, and the moment their mission was accomplished at
any given place, Hashem instructed them to move on.

Thus, the time that Bnei Yisrael spent camping at any given location
was just a means to an end. It served as a preparation for the moment
of departure. It softened the opposition of the forces of evil, and, with
their departure, Bnei Yisrael wrenched away control of the holy sparks.
At other times, their mere passing through a place was enough for them
to take ownership of whatever sparks were scattered there.

---

15 *Bamidbar* 33:1.

Hence, the Torah's focus is on the travels, which indeed were the very point of their wanderings.

LIFE LESSON

What is down but brings us up?

Downtime, of course.

Having some downtime has always been appreciated as beneficial for us and a means to spur our productivity. Nonstop work is a sure recipe for burnout, lowered productivity, and diminished creativity, and it could snuff out one's very vitality.

Killing time is distantly related to utilizing downtime. The two bear some resemblance but are very different in reality. In the past, the sport of killing time was reserved for the nobility, who had lots of money and time to waste. This unhealthy union of unlimited resources and boredom spawned many offspring, collectively known as the entertainment industry.

This idea of killing time is not such a novelty anymore and is no longer the exclusive property of imperial courts and noble patrons. The entertainment industry readily caters to anyone who feels noble at heart. In fact, in all probability, we've all enjoyed our fair share of this once royal treat.

In more recent times, the two distant cousins (the downtime of the simple folk and the time-killing of the nobility) have merged into a single new entity simply known as leisure. Leisure encompasses everything done for enjoyment during our free time and is employed to fill downtime and to kill time. Leisure is a new idea, a new ideology, and a new industry.

To the untrained eye the two do appear very similar, so why shouldn't they merge into one? However, in reality, these two alternative uses of time could not be more disparate. The essential purpose of downtime is to increase productivity by recharging our batteries. Using downtime indicates an appreciation for time, since the ultimate goal is to maximize our productivity, thereby accomplishing more in less time. Killing time, however, shows the opposite — a lack of appreciation for the value of time. Since the coinage of the term leisure, the boundaries between the two have become blurred. While we are involved in what we convince ourselves is the virtuous activity of leisure, we don't allow ourselves to feel guilt for allowing our precious time to die an untimely and cruel death.

Yet while we agree that leisure is important — it keeps us going, it recharges our batteries — indulging in it too much can also potentially drain our batteries once the recharge is complete. Too much leisure, and we might start liking it too much, to the point that it weakens our inner drive.

We surely can't afford to have a leisurely attitude about leisure. With such a fine line separating the healthy downtime leisure from the unhealthy time-killing leisure, how can we be careful not to cross the line?

It might be difficult, but it's not impossible. We need only keep our focus on what we stand to gain from our travels, trips, and other leisure activities. When there's a clear benefit, such as preventing burnout, refreshing ourselves, spending quality time with family, etc., then we can consider it a truly worthwhile endeavor. However, if the only benefit it affords us is to pass the time, then we have effectively assassinated our best friend — time.

Moniker or not, leisure for the sake of leisure is pointless. When we attempt to kill time, we are in essence investing enormous amounts of effort and money to eliminate something that would disappear on its own, without any outside intervention. How foolish an endeavor!

Leisure is important. Let's not waste it by killing time!

GET PAST THAT CLOSED DOOR!

The country was in a state of disarray. Corruption was rampant at every level of government. Complaining to the higher-ups about corruption at the lower levels of government was pointless, as all officials were equally corrupt. The citizens suffered in silence; they had no other choice. If only the king would be made aware of what was going on he would surely do something to prevent his country from destroying itself. Alas, the king's guards were in cahoots with the corrupt ministers, and in fact were themselves thieves and murderers. Anyone whom they suspected of enlightening the king of the situation was not allowed into the palace.

One man wasn't ready to just suffer in silence. He devised a plan to get to the king. He worked slowly and methodically, building up a trustful relationship with the guards. He spent a lot of time in their company, and he showered them with gifts. Once he gained the trust of the guards, he went to the king and described to him the true state of the country. The king quickly set about investigating the matter, and he implemented sweeping reforms to the system.[16]

TORAH LESSON

When the Torah describes the actions of a *ben sorer u'moreh*, it includes the son's disregard for his parents and their orders. The Torah uses the terminology *einenu* to describe how doesn't listen to his parents. The Ohr HaChaim explains that the Torah's use of this term implies that the wayward son is barred from listening to his parents.[17] Not only does he not listen to his parents, he cannot listen to them, because when a person enthrones the *yetzer hara* within himself he can no longer listen to what is said to him.

The *yetzer hara* stands at the doorway of the heart and blocks all words from penetrating since he is well aware that once words of Torah and reason enter a person's heart he, the *yetzer hara*, will no longer be welcome. So he stands vigil and does not allow any such words to enter.

LIFE LESSON

Why can't we taste the sweetness of success? Why is it that we so often stand at the threshold of success only to find our entrance barred by a locked door? We can see it and smell it, but we can't touch it. How frustrating it is to see success just beyond our reach!

What is it that blocks our path to success? Why indeed is it so beyond our reach?

We may encounter this closed door on many of the roads that we travel:

---

16   Based on a parable of the Ohr HaChaim, *Devarim* 21:18.
17   Ibid.

- When we want to improve our social standing and have more friends.
- When we wish to implement all the great organizational skills we've heard and read about.
- When we desire to awaken earlier but can't resist the urge to hit the snooze button.
- When we have every intention to start a new project but can't fight procrastination.
- When our weight on the scale reads like numbers on a tax bill, yet the diet just never happens.

Why? Why is the sweet taste of success barred to us?

Oftentimes, we feel stuck in a situation, prevented from advancing toward success. We wonder why others are succeeding while we're stuck. What is their formula for success while we seem only to meet failure? Of course, we know that everything is from Hashem, but we want to understand what it is that obstructs our path to success. After all, it's part of our *hishtadlus* obligation to try our best, so what are we doing wrong?

The answer might come as a surprise.

It is very likely that the doors to success have really been open to us, yet we have slammed them shut ourselves — by fearing success itself. This fear holds us back from reaching our potential.

Fear of success often stems from an assumption that if we are to meet success we'll have to live up to higher standards expected of people at such a level of success. Since we're unsure of exactly what these standards are, we choose to stay where we are rather than greet success that may demand change. This irrational fear stands guard at the door of our hearts and doesn't allow any suggestions for success to enter.

- We might be afraid to start socializing more because we're afraid of possible rejection.
- We could be afraid to become more organized for fear of the pressure we'll feel to stay organized.

- We may fear feeling tired the entire day and thus not follow through with our plan to rise earlier.
- We might procrastinate starting a project out of fear that it'll be too difficult, or that it won't be good enough.
- We ignore the numbers on the scale because we're terrified of being hungry or never again being able to indulge.

This is amazing news, because it means there are not countless doors closing on us. Only one door is — our very own inner door that fears success. Additionally, it is within our means to get a hold of the key to open our inner door, if only we identify what is blocking us and find a way to get around it. How encouraging!

A word of caution: Fear is a feeling and feelings are irrational by nature. It is pointless to rationalize with irrational feelings, and it would be inadvisable to engage in open battle in order to get past them and into our hearts. Rather than try to convince ourselves that our fears are nonsensical, we should accept the fears and even form an alliance with them. By recognizing that we have subconsciously produced these fears as a means of protection, we can accept them while choosing not to dwell on these feelings. The fears come from a place of misguided love of ourselves, a love that doesn't want us to get hurt.

When we hear the voices of fear and uncertainty in our heads, we can talk back to ourselves and tell our fears that we appreciate their services. We could tell them that we love them and accept them. After all they did have our best interests in mind. Give credit where credit is due!

Afterwards, we can tell ourselves that right now we're just not in the mood of thinking and dwelling on our feelings. We might still feel some apprehension and we'll possibly still hear the voice of reluctance, but that's fine. So long as we remember that, we won't be so bothered by their company.

To be fair — and to help quiet these fearful thoughts — we can set up designated worry zones, consisting of five- to ten-minute periods a few times a day to do nothing else but dwell on our worries. As soon as the time is up, so is our worrying, until the next break.

As soon as we open our inner door we'll find that many previously closed doors will open for us.

The only limits to our achievements and accomplishments are the limits we place upon ourselves!

BREAK FREE FROM LUST'S STRANGLEHOLD!

Major corporations spend billions of dollars in the research of psychology. The money does not come from their charity funds, nor are their intentions to further the understanding of the human mind. The research is all about marketing, to better understand the weaknesses of people in order to ensnare them with the right advertisements.

These researchers have zeroed in on the workings of our psyche. When we feel attracted to an advertisement it's not because we like the product, but because we've been sucked into a well-orchestrated plot. Frightening as it sounds, we are, to a large degree, not acting of our own free will. Rather, our reactions have been predetermined by the marketing experts.

The secret to their successful stranglehold over us lies in their ability to harness the major forces of lust, desire, and insecurity within us. The advertisements communicate with our subconscious minds, convincing us the advertised product or service will satisfy our lust, fulfill our desires, and remove our insecurities. Very often, a combination of more than one power is at work. And while we convince ourselves that our decisions were made rationally, in reality we are no more than manipulated pawns!

TORAH LESSON

In discussing the incredible power of lust, the Ohr HaChaim says that, generally, every commandment from Hashem is within human power to fulfill — that is, aside from the prohibition against inappropriate lust.[18] The only way to overcome the seductive power of lust is to refrain from even a single inappropriate sight or thought.

A lone sight or thought is enough to cast a seductive spell upon the victim. Following that, the battle is an uphill one and tilted to one's disadvantage. One could argue that this prohibition was only intended for those who have never crossed the bridge, because once crossed there is no going back.

But the Torah lets us know that all is not lost. As Yidden, our close relationship with Hashem serves as a counterforce, and this knowledge can anchor us; when we begin to feel drawn toward lust, we can will ourselves to think of Hashem's closeness, and the troublesome emotions will disappear. True, it may not be so easy, but no matter our history, it's always possible to apply the brakes and change course. Living a life of sanctity is within reach for anyone willing to apply himself!

LIFE LESSON

What has a stronger pull than even the greatest magnet?

18   *Vayikra* 18:2.

Lust! It has such an immense drawing power that nothing can stop it. Neither massive walls nor great distances can diminish the seductive power of lust! Very often, one cannot even be sure how it started; it may have been a sight, a sound, or a fleeting thought. But that is irrelevant while a burning desire flares within and must be overcome. A victim of the intensity of lust feels possessed, unable to think of anything else. This force doesn't allow for rational thought as the raging fire within consumes a person bit by bit.

Any attempt to drown this fiery lust in a sea of other thoughts is met with failure, and it returns with an even greater viciousness. Running away is equally unsuccessful; the lustful thoughts just follow, buoyed by the wind of one's running. Every attempt to crush these thoughts fails; they just gain strength through the struggle. Lust laughs the person in the face knowing that it's got the victim in its stranglehold.

Facing these repeated failures should one just give up? Should one allow the fire to rage unchecked, to burn him to a cinder?

No! There is hope.

Let's take an inside look at our operating systems to see how we can stop the lust virus from destroying us. We generally operate in what's known as the cognitive triangle. The three sides that make up this triangle are thoughts, emotions, and behaviors.

When a virus enters our system it sets the triangle moving. A sight, sound, or memory will cause us to think in a certain direction. These thoughts then stimulate our emotions, which reinforce our thoughts, and can then easily lead to an action (behavior). One foreign bug can activate this triangle and send it spiraling—like a wheel spinning out of control—and we can easily lose our balance.

The easiest time to take action is when we detect the first tingling of lust. As long as the virus hasn't contaminated our entire operating system the triangle is much easier to grab hold of and control.

We can boost our strength by keeping in mind that we're part of something much greater and much more powerful than the seductiveness of lust. We have our closeness to Hashem and He has trust in us! This thought will give us the boost we need to overcome the seductiveness of lust and will lead to positive feelings of empowerment. The more we think this thought, the more we will feel it. We'll then have the capability to direct our behaviors in a meaningful and constructive way.

We can also attempt to stop the wheel by thinking other empowering thoughts and by running in the opposite direction or purposely distracting ourselves. However, that will only truly work when we connect with Hashem and feel His closeness. Lust is fire and is best fought with the fire of our closeness to Hashem!

Hashem has given us the elusive key we need to gain control over this formidable challenge. Let's use it!

Let's not settle for being pawns; we are meant to be kings!

GRAB THAT OPPORTUNITY!

B rokenhearted and barefoot, the procession made its way quietly through the countryside. The great king who had fearlessly conquered country after country was now a fugitive in his own land. Uncertainty and dread prevailed among the group. No one knew what to expect; there was no way to know how the rebellion would end. It was the lowest point in the turbulent life of their beloved and courageous leader.

Suddenly, they passed a respected and familiar fellow: the personal tutor of the crown prince. However, he had not come to offer solace and encouragement to his benefactor the king at this desperate time of need. Quite the contrary, he deridingly showered the procession with mud and pebbles accompanied by choice insults. The king's guards wished to administer punishment to the ingrate, but the king stopped them and said, "Hashem told him to curse."

David HaMelech asked Hashem to be mentioned in davening along with the Patriarchs; this was his lifelong aspiration. When Hashem told him that they had all withstood difficult tests and he hadn't, David asked Hashem to be tested. Hashem told him he'll be tested and he'll fail. This was followed by the story of Bas Sheva, which was his test, and, predictably, David failed.[19]

It was at this lowest point in his life that David HaMelech achieved his greatest heights. At that moment, he was granted his lifelong dream: Hashem was hence called *Magen David*. David had withstood many *nisyonos* in his life, yet none had fulfilled this dream. With this test, however, his wish was finally granted.[20]

TORAH LESSON

Hashem informed Moshe that due to his sin at *mei merivah* he would not merit to lead Bnei Yisrael into Eretz Yisrael. The Ohr HaChaim takes issue with this.[21] Hadn't Hashem already informed Moshe by the *sneh* and at other occasions that he wouldn't be the one to lead Bnei Yisrael into Eretz Yisrael?

The Ohr HaChaim answers that the primary reason Moshe was barred from entering Eretz Yisrael was so that he wouldn't build the Beis Hamikdash. Because were he to build it, the holiness embedded in the building would prevent it from ever being destroyed. In the event that Klal Yisrael would sin, Hashem wouldn't be able to vent His anger on the Beis Hamikdash, and the Yidden would bear the brunt of His fury. Hashem, therefore, prevented Moshe from entering Eretz Yisrael.

---

19 *Sanhedrin* 107a.
20 Rabbi Avigdor Miller, *Am Segulah Vol. I*, paragraphs 442–443.
21 *Bamidbar* 20:8.

However, says the Ohr HaChaim, Moshe had a great opportunity to change the course of history. Had Moshe followed Hashem's ruling and spoken to the rock the *kiddush Hashem* would have been enormous. It would have left such a lasting impression on Bnei Yisrael that they would never have sinned again, leaving no reason for Hashem to ever pour His wrath upon wood and stone. Moshe would have built the Beis Hamikdash and it would have stood for eternity while everyone served Hashem properly. By striking the rock, Moshe forfeited a rare opportunity and his fate was sealed.

LIFE LESSON

Oh, how many times do we feel like we just want to give up!

The obstacles we face seem too difficult to surmount. We have withstood many trials and stayed strong in the face of challenges, but now it feels like too much! How many times do we have to prove ourselves? Haven't we been tested enough? Can't we throw in the towel and admit defeat? If we haven't succeeded until this point, why should we believe that the situation will ever change and we'll ever succeed?

One may have invested so much into trying to help his child with an issue he is struggling with. He spent countless hours consulting professionals, trying every variety of in-the-box and out-of-the-box approaches and methods. He's held discussions with the principal and *rebbi* — with little results. He spent a small fortune and a great deal of time and effort, yet there are no measurable improvements. He's ready to call it quits. Why spend more time and effort to try another approach? Why believe that this one will be any more successful than its numerous predecessors?

You've been searching for a *parnassah* for so long. You've sent out your résumé to countless potential employers and sat through many long and sometimes humiliating interviews, only to be rejected time and again. You feel dejected and worthless and have lost all impetus to try again. Why subject your fractured and deflated ego to additional beatings? But with much coaching from your spouse you gather the courage to give it one more shot. This opportunity definitely sounds promising.

You arrive at the interview and are made to wait an indefinite amount of time. Whatever confidence you had left melted into an ugly puddle right there in the waiting room. Then, at the actual interview, the boss looks and speaks so condescendingly it makes you doubt your own intelligence. He then informs you, in his ultra-patronizing tone, that there are surely companies out there who'd appreciate your talents. You stumble out of the office, face burning in shame, heart throbbing from indignation. Hadn't you known it was a waste to try? You feel like an utter loser!

Your feelings are surely justified. You've worked hard to earn your membership at the Losers' Club, where you can keep company with other unfortunate losers. However, before you step through the club's formidable doors, remember that the club affords its members no opportunities; you can only lose out by joining. So what's the point? Instead, continue to knock on doors. One of them might just be the door to opportunity!

When we find ourselves in a situation of the proverbial straw that breaks the camel's back, let's remember that we are not camels! We humans were created with the amazing ability to stretch the limits of our endurance!

We never know when the opportune moment will arrive. Just because it hasn't worked out until now doesn't mean that we are failures. It simply hasn't yet been the right time. If we give up, we surely won't reach our goal, but if we hang on, we just might!

The thorn we've just encountered might be the
final one before reaching the rose!

HAIL TO THE CHIEF

Mr. Kleinman was thrilled. Life was starting to look up. If things would only continue this way, he'd soon be able to cast off the inferiority complex that had been hounding him since his childhood. His rise had been meteoric and he had catapulted up the social ladder like a shooting star. His new status meant that others looked up at him. This sensation was totally new for him and he drank it all in with an insatiable thirst.

Mr. Kleinman loved his new star status and was terrified to lose it. He made sure to keep his opinions in line with whatever was popular at the time, and when styles shifted, he changed his opinions to match. In short, Mr. Kleinman was hooked on popularity and he held on to it steadfastly.

Soon enough, people started becoming annoyed with Mr. Kleinman's weakness of character. They felt they could not count on his honesty and that there was little substance to him.

It seemed nothing was too valuable for Mr. Kleinman to sacrifice for the sake of his popularity, and to his utter devastation, Mr. Kleinman's circle of admirers began to shrink rapidly.

TORAH LESSON

Reuven, the firstborn son of Yaakov Avinu, should have received the kingship as his birthright. Why then was the kingship given to Yehuda? The Ohr HaChaim says Yehuda was awarded the kingship for being the first person to publicly confess his misdeeds.[22] Although Chazal tell us that Reuven was the first person to repent, it didn't earn him the kingship — for he did so in private and didn't have the courage to publicly confess.[23] It was only after Yehuda's courageous public confession that Reuven followed suit.

Thus, we see that leadership is not about knowing what's right, but about being courageous and following one's convictions even when they are not popular. Reuven knew he had done wrong, and he repented; but Yehuda placed a lot on the line with his public confession — yet he did it anyway, because he knew it was the right thing. Now, that is courage! That is the sign of a true leader!

LIFE LESSON

What's the world's most popular contest?

The popularity contest, of course!

Many of us are contestants in this contest. We compete in it, investing and sacrificing in the hope to win.

What is it about this popularity contest that gets us all worked up?

For starters, it feels good to be popular! Popularity teases us with its dazzle and excitement. We are enticed by the twinkling of the stars and we stand in awe of great personalities. We too want to taste the joy of popularity. Simple enough, isn't it? But there is something more profound to it.

22	*Bereishis* 49:3-4.
23	*Bereishis Rabbah* 84:18.

As humans we are conditioned to engage in the guessing game, constantly double guessing ourselves, insecure with our decisions and actions. This self-doubt gnaws at our innards and makes us feel awful. We search desperately for some reassurance, and popularity seems to promise us this. Popularity is easily confused with validation, so we decide we're okay when we become popular. So what if we don't really believe in ourselves? Others do, and we've got to have faith in their judgment!

But is popularity really worthwhile?

Possibly, but the road to get there is a treacherous one. The popularity contest is a very dangerous sport. Many a contestant has fallen victim to character assassination in the process of winning the contest. At times, we knowingly, or unknowingly, place our true character in jeopardy in order to become popular. We sacrifice some of our values to obtain the worthless glitter of popularity. What an unfair exchange!

It also pays to remember that, sometimes, those twinkling stars are no more than a bunch of noxious gasses. Do we want to style ourselves into glamorous shells with hollow insides?

The need for validation is a real one, but we need not engage in star-gazing to fill it. We can obtain it through a different and more solid approach — by becoming leaders! We could thrive on the sense of fulfillment that comes from leadership. How do we accomplish that? If the popularity contest is dangerous, isn't the presidential election much more so?

The truth is, we're not talking about the superficial aspect of leadership. We are speaking of true leadership, which consists of the determination to act upon our convictions even when they're not so popular! Leadership is about blazing a path and leading the way. And it need not be on a grand scale. Whenever a leader sees a need, he takes the initiative. How empowering!

Yes, we all have it within ourselves to be leaders and to bring about positive change, be it on a small scale or on a larger one. Why forgo the opportunity to hone our leadership skills? Let's jump right in!

True, our actions won't always win us the popularity contest, but they will define us as true leaders. We'll become the leaders of our own lives, and the inner satisfaction that we'll feel will be our best validation.

Leadership is about following our convictions, not others' opinions!

HAVE THE CAKE, EAT IT, ENJOY IT!

The Gold's Shabbos *sheva brachos* was the talk of town. Those lucky enough to be invited had the time of their lives. The event even outshone the actual wedding. It took place at an exclusive resort and, for the duration of their stay, all the guests were treated as royalty. They were showered with gifts ranging from a beautiful *kiddush* cup to a number of *sefarim* and cute trinkets for the kids. The food was great and the program spectacular.

The Greens were not originally on the invitation list. However, at the last minute, the caterer procured them an invitation as his personal friends. They felt privileged to attend and were especially overjoyed with the numerous treats and gifts. They couldn't have wished for a better getaway.

However, throughout the Shabbos, whenever anyone questioned them about their connection to the *baalei simchah*, they would quietly answer that they were actually guests of the caterer. How humbling that was. Even later on, whenever they made use of the gifts they had received, they always remembered the discomfort they had felt at being "uninvited" guests. They had the cake, and they ate it, but they didn't enjoy it!

TORAH LESSON

Hashem promised the *Avos* that He would give Eretz Yisrael to their descendants. As Bnei Yisrael prepared to enter Eretz Yisrael, Moshe made it clear to them that it wasn't in their merit they were being granted the land. It was only a fulfillment of Hashem's promise to our forefathers. True, Bnei Yisrael were righteous at that point, but they weren't worthy enough to merit receiving the land in their own right.

Moshe instructed Bnei Yisrael on the proper protocol for crossing the *Yarden*. He said, "And it will be on that day that you will cross the *Yarden* to the land that Hashem your Lord is giving you; and you shall erect large boulders and plaster them. And you shall write upon them this Torah when you cross over in order that you may enter the land that Hashem your Lord is giving to you."[24]

The Ohr HaChaim explains that Moshe was informing Bnei Yisrael that by fulfilling this mitzvah they'd become worthy of receiving the land in their own merit — and not just in the merit of *Avos*.

While it was the same land that they'd be receiving, following Moshe's instructions created a totally different concept!

LIFE LESSON

Who doesn't enjoy a freebie?

Aren't we all thrilled to get things for free? But, alas, the excitement doesn't last, as freebies tend to have less value in our eyes. We naturally

---

24   *Devarim* 27:2-3.

cherish and appreciate things more when we have worked hard to obtain them. We'll even value something small more than something big if we worked hard for the small item and received the big one for free.

Let's be objective — few could object to the thrill of accumulating objects. In fact, we're almost possessed by our desire to accumulate possessions. When our moods are down, we turn to shopping therapy to lift our spirits. When we're happy, we complement our mood with some positive shopping. And when we just chance upon something nice, we also convince ourselves that we deserve it and we make the purchase.

This holds true in relation to ourselves and to our offspring as well. We oftentimes express our love to our children through objects. When we spot something we believe our kids would enjoy, we feel a strong urge to purchase it for them. Oh, how wonderful we feel when our children's faces light up with an appreciative smile as we hand them a new toy or gadget. It makes the purchase price well worth it.

While indulgence affords us a rush of momentary excitement, the thrill wears off rather quickly, especially if the purchase wasn't really necessary. However, were we to work hard in order to procure something, it would be so much more valuable for us, as we derive considerably more enjoyment from something we've worked hard to earn, as mentioned above. If instead of indulging our every whim, we made ourselves earn each purchase, we could get so much more excitement from our acquisitions.

But how can we suddenly start earning rewards? We're out in the real world, and no one is giving out points or arranging award programs.

With no alternative, we should do it ourselves! We are each aware of our own personal weaknesses, of the places we fall short, and have a long list of habits that we would love to change. Very often we try to improve, but we fall short of our goal. So why not create an incentive program to motivate us, to get that little extra push we need?

Come up with a plan to reward yourself for every challenge you set for yourself. Once you've accumulated enough money, you can allow yourself to purchase the item you've wanted. With this you will accomplish two things: You will succeed in working on areas of improvement more easily, and you will get greater pleasure out of your purchases. Instead of indulging, you'll be enjoying well-earned rewards. A win-win situation!

The same holds true with our children. We can always find some area for them to improve, and then they can receive the item they wanted as a reward, and they'll cherish it so much more!

Our most cherished reward is knowing that we deserved our reward!

LIVE IN THE PRESENT!

D r. Gordio, a disciple of the *Maggid* of Mezritch, was a *baal teshuvah* who had spent his early years as a court physician for the king of Prussia. Dr. Gordio once complained to his *rebbi* that he was occasionally bothered by immoral thoughts, a throwback to his previous lifestyle. The *maggid* shared with him the following story.

Chaim, the village's tavern keeper, suffered terribly from the local drunkards. They would loiter in his tavern for hours on end and use vile language, often getting quite rowdy. As his daughters started to get older, Chaim decided it was necessary to close down the tavern to shield his daughters from the negative influences of the coarse drunkards. It took some time for the drunkards to finally accept that the tavern was closed for good. Every once in a while, though, a drunkard would come by and demand a drink. Chaim would very firmly tell the drunkard that he had come to the wrong place and that the tavern was no longer open. He left no room for additional pleas or arguments.

"You," the *rebbi* told Dr. Gordio, "are like that tavern keeper. Just because you were once the address for the drunkards, the immoral thoughts, doesn't mean you always have to be. When those decadent thoughts come to haunt you, just tell them that you've changed, that you are not the right address anymore."

TORAH LESSON

"And now Yisrael, what is Hashem your G-d requesting from you, only to fear Hashem your G-d."[25] The Ohr HaChaim quotes a Chazal that defines the word *v'atah*, and now, as a reference to *teshuvah*. The Torah is informing us that in order to repent we need only one thing: fear of Hashem.[26] Why would the word "now" be a reference to *teshuvah*, repentance? In order to understand this, let's take a closer look at the idea of *teshuvah*.

Generally, we all want to do what's right and it bothers us greatly when we slip up. We want to be better and correct our ways. So why is it that very often we just stay the way we are?

Oftentimes, it's because we feel weighed down by baggage from our past, and we're worried about the future. We have flashbacks and feel as if we'll never be able to sever the ropes tying us to an unpleasant past. We're also afraid of committing ourselves to a new reality, not knowing what the future will bring. Thus, for *teshuvah* to be successful, we need to focus on the present and not on the weight of the past or the worry of the future.

LIFE LESSON

How often do we attempt to change only to fail again?

---

25   *Devarim* 10:12.
26   *Bereishis Rabbah* 21:6.

Too often! We easily feel flustered and lost when we repeatedly commit to change and then don't succeed. Déjà vu is our motto, and we become disheartened when we notice how many changes we've hoped to implement but haven't accomplished.

Why, indeed, do we keep on failing? There are many possibilities:

- It's possible that while we want to change, we don't have a clear plan for what to do, so we don't do anything at all.
- It's also likely that we try to bite off too much at once — more than we can chew and digest — so we give up.

But there are plenty of times when we do take the proper precautions — we don't take too big of a jump, we have a good plan of action — yet we still fail.

Does this mean that we're failures? Certainly not.

It's quite possible that we're simply not mentally present when it's time to make the change. Very often just as we're about to make a change, we take a detour down memory lane. We lose ourselves in the memories of our past difficulties and shortcomings. We relive all our letdowns and failures. We become so lost in the past that we can't find our way back to the present. We feel overwhelmed by our colorful history!

At other times, we decide to venture into the future. We begin to imagine how we'll look as new and different people. We try to connect with that image of the new us when we suddenly get stricken with stranger anxiety! We'll never feel comfortable around the new us! We decide to stick to the familiar and predictable. Why should we risk discomfort?

Thus, change is neither for historians nor for futuristic explorers. True change can only take place in the present. It's not all that difficult to make a change today. Once we were successful today, we can try to replicate it tomorrow. If it didn't work so well today, that has no bearing on tomorrow.

We need only concentrate on what to do now, at this moment. Reminiscing about the past can be a fun activity, but it has no bearing on what we can accomplish now. When our thoughts involuntarily wander to the past, we can remind ourselves that right now we're not studying history. We are too busy living in the present.

The same holds true with our worrying over the future. Leave the worrying to bigwigs in Washington D.C. They get paid to worry about any problem that may potentially hit us in the future. We're not getting paid to do that so why should we waste precious time and effort on such a useless endeavor? Let's leave the worrying to the experts!

Make the most of the present; in a moment it'll already be history!

MASTER YOUR OWN LOVE

aniel was depressed and full of self-loathing. In his mid-forties, he had a nice family and a stable job, but that did little to make him feel positive. He saw himself as a total failure and unworthy of love and happiness. Life was one long chain of negativity and bleakness. When he had attempted to draw up a list of things that he could be happy about and love himself for he came up blank. Love was something that was not meant for him. He didn't deserve it.

Daniel was fed up with his self-hate and was determined to rise above it. He invested a lot of time and effort searching within himself for even a minor positive trait. It was tedious labor, but ever so slowly, Daniel succeeded in finding reasons why he was worthy of love, and he eventually learned how to provide himself with that love.

TORAH LESSON

The Ohr HaChaim takes issue with the Torah's command to love Hashem.[27] He asks, how can it be demanded of us to love Hashem? How can we control whom — or Whom — we love? He then offers an amazing three-pronged approach to taking control of our love.

Reframe: We can reframe our relationship with Hashem. If we focus on how Hashem went to great lengths to ensure that we'd be His privileged nation, it will create within us an awareness of the enormous privilege we have of being close to Him. If we were to combine all the pleasures of the world, it would not equal the incredible sweetness of dwelling in the embrace of Hashem's love. Nothing can be more attractive than a loving relationship with the very Source of joy and pleasure!

Refocus: No matter how positive we are, we will inevitably feel dragged down by certain hardships in life. When we focus on those hardships we could easily become distracted. This distraction could in turn, lessen our feelings of closeness to Hashem, and when that happens it's time to refocus. It's time to remind ourselves of our fabulous and exciting treasure — our closeness to Hashem. If someone is short on cash but owns an enormous diamond, he surely doesn't feel like a pauper. In the same vein, when we're in the embrace of infinite love, we can more easily handle life's challenges.

Reaffirm: The final element necessary to build a solid foundation of love of Hashem is to constantly take time to focus on all the benefits of being close to Hashem. The more time we spend thinking about it, the stronger our bond will become.

Those three Rs are the keys that will afford us control over our emotions. By properly implementing the above three steps, we can gain control over our love. Hence, it is well within the confines of our ability to master love of Hashem.

LIFE LESSON

What is the most powerful emotion?

---

27   *Devarim* 6:5–6.

Love!

Love can obstruct reason. It has the power to build and to destroy. It drives mankind to its greatest heights and, conversely, to its lowest depths. Philosophers and psychologists have theorized about its secrets, attempting to harness its potency.

We stand in reverence to it and feel like we have no control over it. How often do we wish to access it but discover that it is beyond our reach? We want to love, but we have no idea how to. After all, isn't it impossible to force an emotion?

Love may be powerful, it may be a dominant emotion, but it is not beyond our control. True, reason flies out the window when love comes through the door. However, we have the key to the door, and we can choose whether or not to allow love to enter.

What is the key?

The key to our emotions is our thoughts. Emotions do not happen on their own — they are the products of our thoughts. Positive thoughts bring on positive emotions, and negative thoughts cause negative emotions. It's that simple!

Now that we have the key, we must learn how to use it.

All too often we fall into the trap of self-hate. We hate ourselves for our looks, for the way we treat others, for our eating habits, for our shortcomings. The list is endless! We continuously berate ourselves for our deficiencies, hoping it will motivate us to improve. But, alas, it doesn't seem to work. The more we dwell on our shortcomings, the more inadequacies we notice. The more we notice, the more we hate ourselves, and the lower our moods drop. With all this self-hate, we're quite understandably not in a position to improve. Who would want to help someone he hates so strongly?

We hate ourselves for hating ourselves but we don't know how to access that elusive self-love. So, for lack of anything better, we continue to self-destruct through self-hate.

This must stop! We do have access to self-love! Let's follow the three steps laid out so beautifully by the Ohr HaChaim (and "discovered" by modern psychology), and we'll be able to master the art of creating and cultivating love.

Reframe: You are definitely not all negative! Find something good about yourself — an attribute or a deed. It may be useful to make a list of the things you like about yourself. Recall all the times you made a positive impact on others, the times you overcame a weakness. Don't view this exercise as a chore that will magically change the way you feel. Rather, spend time thinking about the traits and actions you write down, and dwell on them, allowing yourself to feel good about them.

Refocus: There will be times when you'll find yourself feeling down and negative about yourself. Rather than attempt to fight the mood, take out the list you wrote up and focus on the positive attributes you have. There is so much good you can think about. When done correctly, the negativity will slowly disappear, because it's too difficult to maintain a negative mood while thinking positive thoughts.

Reaffirm: Regularly spend as much time as possible thinking about the good things in your life. Think about your good qualities and about the many good deeds you've done — big or small. Once you get used to thinking good thoughts about yourself, you'll find more reasons to like yourself.

By following the three Rs, our self-hate will dissipate. It'll be replaced by a deep sense of self-love. With the new self-love in place, we'll find it much easier to work on our self-enhancement, which will give us more reason to love ourselves. We'll also learn to love ourselves despite our shortcomings. Yes, we can and should love ourselves. We deserve it!

We can invite loving thoughts in through the door,
and self-hate will fly out the window!

REDISTRIBUTION OF
WEALTH?

M r. G. was euphoric! Late Uncle Mike's attorney had just notified him that he'd been listed as one of the beneficiaries of his childless uncle's sizeable estate. Now that was something to be excited about! His portion of the inheritance was enough to set him up comfortably.

Mr. G. was not unaware of the reactions of others when they heard of his good fortune. Friends and strangers alike had a hard time concealing their envy as they congratulated him. Many were openly hostile and voiced their suspicions that Mr. G. had employed some foul play to obtain the fortune. Others believed that it was Mr. G.'s moral obligation to share his windfall with those less fortunate than he. Before long, Mr. G. sensed resentment surrounding him; his acquaintances just didn't seem to think that his new status was fair.

There is no denying it — people possess an innate desire for fairness!

TORAH LESSON

When discussing some of the monetary misdemeanors between man and his fellow man — such as taking unlawful possession of someone else's belongings — the Torah terms it "an embezzlement from Hashem."[28] This choice of terminology seems out of place, as there is no reference to *hekdesh* property in this *pasuk*.

The Ohr HaChaim explains that, indeed, when a person steals or takes possession of another's property unlawfully, he is guilty of embezzling from Hashem, as he is disrupting Hashem's will. Hashem had deemed one person worthy of a given item or sum of money for reasons beyond our grasp. When a thief or schemer relieves this person of his possession, he is interfering with Hashem's judgment and plan. Thus, he is considered embezzling from Hashem, even if he justifies his actions based on fairness.

LIFE LESSON

Why do people have so many problems? Why is there so much misery in the world?

Because we invite misery!

Misery is caused mostly by ourselves and very little, if at all, by others. If we find ourselves feeling miserable often, it's probably our own fault. When you search for ways you've been shortchanged you're likely to end up miserable, because your innate sense of fairness gets ruffled when you perceive such injustice.

- We can't understand why the family down the block is extremely wealthy while we can't even make ends

---

28 *Vayikra* 5:21.

meet. Couldn't there be a more equal distribution of wealth?

- With hearts full of pain, we reflect on how much we're struggling with our children while our neighbors are reaping truckloads of *nachas*.
- Someone who isn't nearly as qualified as you are lands the job that you so coveted!
- The school accepted some families much less appropriate for their parent body than you, while your family was rejected
- We watch painfully as the conniving and dishonest seem to make it while the straightforward and honest people struggle.

Where is justice? Where is fairness? Don't we deserve to have things a little better?

Not only do we detect injustices that make us feel miserable, we seem to even create them! Sometimes we're actually feeling quite happy and satisfied until we spot someone who we believe has more than we do. Suddenly, our contentment vanishes, leaving nary a trace. It's a disappearing act as powerful as black magic. When the other succeeds, it somehow magically wipes away everything we have, and our world goes black.

If we would just think about it logically we'd realize that this thought process makes absolutely no sense! Why do we suddenly have less just because others have more? Nothing has actually changed, yet we allow ourselves to feel so miserable.

We could allow ourselves to be sucked into this magical black hole and write ourselves off as a modern-day casualty of black magic. But do we really want that? Do we really enjoy spending so much time in the company of our misery?

We spend so much time volunteering for the World Fairness Fighters Organization. We're busy looking out for all the unfairness, especially in our personal lives. It takes up so much of our precious time and the only reward we receive is a generous dose of heartache. What for? No one is going to reimburse us for all the complaining — and it was hard work!

Let's instead invest our resources in a much more rewarding endeavor. Misery is generally caused by looking away from ourselves and focusing on and calculating other people's assets and feeling miserable about it. Let's start looking into ourselves and review our own assets instead. Let's start spending some time dwelling on all the good things that we have in life. We may not have recognized it before, but we each have many things to be happy about. The more time we'll spend on introspection, the more adept we'll become at realizing just how much good we actually have.

Those out there who are still loyally volunteering for the World Fairness Fighters Organization might even be looking at us and feeling that our lives are much better than theirs. How unfair!

There does exist a fear that by focusing on the good we have, we won't have anything to complain about, or we'll feel uncomfortable complaining since we have so much good. This fear is a valid one and we thus must choose the lesser of the two evils.

When we feel life is being unfair, it might just be that our sense of fairness is off balance!

RID YOURSELF OF
NEGATIVITY

R' Yitzchak was an accomplished *talmid chacham*. Though only in his early thirties, he had already acquired a depth and breadth of knowledge comparable to scholars many years his senior. However, R' Yitzchak couldn't appreciate his accomplishments; he was too full of negativity toward himself. He did not have a single positive thing to say about himself — or about anyone else for that matter. Wherever he looked, R' Yitzchak saw only the negative. Everything and everyone was shallow and full of bluff.

His negativity and disapproval of others afforded R' Yitzchak a warped sense of superiority over those around him. He felt he was the only one really striving for perfection and true depth. His negativity toward himself was fueled by his belief that the only way to accomplish his goals was by being overly harsh on himself.

R' Yitzchak really wanted to hold on to this worldview, he just had one side issue he had to take care of. He was getting splitting headaches every day during learning. He thought he would break down from the extreme tension in his life, and he had no real friends. Otherwise, everything was great. Ironically, he saw no connection between his life's outlook and the way he was feeling.

TORAH LESSON

The nation of Midian and their Moabite cronies wrought tremendous pain and damage upon Bnei Yisrael. Hashem commanded Bnei Yisrael to despise the Midianites and to uproot them.[29] The Ohr HaChaim points out that at that point in time Hashem wasn't commanding them to actually make war with Midian. The commandment for war came later. If so, he asks, what was this commandment about?

He explains that Hashem's intention here was for the Jews to uproot their affinity toward Midian. For whoever tastes the flavor of sin — even if only in thought — will find it difficult to separate himself from it. And as long as he has not separated himself from the desire, he will be deprived of atonement. The Jews had tasted obscenity and idolatry, and Hashem wanted to heal them. Hashem thus advised them to hate the provocateurs and to detest any good that came from them. Hashem told Bnei Yisrael to remember the terrible suffering the Midianites had brought upon them. The association of Midian with suffering rather than pleasure, would increase the hatred Bnei Yisrael felt toward them, and would help them sever all emotional ties with Midian. It would help them distance themselves from any thought of sin and to undo any positive association.

---

29   *Bamidbar* 25:17.

LIFE LESSON

We're weighed down by it, we hate it, we dislike others because of it, and it causes us to dislike ourselves as well. What is this awful thing?

Negativity!

With some of us, negativity is such a frequent visitor that we may mistakenly identify it as a close friend or family member. At times, we even find a distorted sense of comfort in the strangling embrace of negativity. It may feel comforting in the moment and we deceive ourselves into believing that we actually enjoy its company. We luxuriate in the soothing feeling negativity affords us.

Negativity has a funny way of making us feel better and "better than." When we are negative about others, we feel better than them. When we are negative about ourselves, we fool ourselves into believing we are exalted truth seekers. This negativity affords us a high! And that's without even imbibing anything. How amazing!

However, not unlike drugs and alcohol, the high we get from negativity is very short lived. Once the positive burst of energy subsides, the full-blown side effects of the negativity tend to set in. We feel so negative about ourselves. We've failed yet again! We're no good! What are we worth if we have no self-control over our negative thoughts? This self-bashing causes us to feel even more negative about ourselves. This spiraling, downhill road can lead us directly into a pit of depression.

We feel ripped apart by our inner struggle. On the one hand, we feel energized and validated by our negativity and we want to hold on to it. But on the other hand, we're aware of the havoc it wreaks within us and we want to get rid of it. We are ready to pay any price to rid ourselves of negativity, except for the price of actually letting go of our negative edge. That's too high a price. This inner fight drives us nuts! It's like we're suffering from multiple personality disorder!

Well, if we do have multiple personalities, why shouldn't we get to know them better? The negative thoughts really are not part of our normal selves. We have our regular selves that strive to be happy and positive. Then we have this perverted negativity that thrives on pessimism and is in cahoots with depression. These two fight within us for dominance and we must adjudicate to determine who will dominate.

If we decide to go with the part of us that likes to be happy and positive, then let's try the following: Let's denounce ownership of and externalize and separate ourselves from the negative thoughts. We can view our negative thoughts as old pesky recordings playing in our minds. It could be bothersome, but no more so than any other background noise.

Once we've externalized these voices and recognized that they are not part of the positive us, we are free to let them go! Why should we hold on to something that's just causing us negativity and making us feel like garbage? We can let go by imagining that we hear those soundtracks playing in our heads and actively reminding ourselves that they're just worthless recordings.

If the negativity feels so at home within us that it refuses to leave, we can learn to get rough with it. We need not be overly accommodating to an enemy who is trying to destroy us! It is okay to get mad at those thoughts and tell them, "Get away from me! Don't bother me; you are not my friend and you don't mean well!" This idea has a proven track record — it really works!

Some of us might balk at the suggestion of self-talk. It could take some getting used to and can be done very discreetly. But it's definitely worth a try, as it's a powerful tool.

Even though negativity can appear to be our friend, we can't allow ourselves to be fooled by its smile — its teeth will bite us!

If we can be negative about positive things, we can surely negate negativity!

THE BEAUTY OF ANGER

Boy was he angry! He felt the heat rise within him and threaten to burn him up from the inside out. He couldn't take the feeling! He desperately needed to blow off some steam even though he knew that it wouldn't be pretty. Yerachmiel's friends were wont to compare him to a volcano. He would constantly simmer and seethe under the surface and every so often there'd be a full-blown explosion that would let loose prodigious amounts of toxic fumes and destructive lava. Many kept their distance from Yerachmiel, as there was no telling when the next explosion would occur.

Yerachmiel hated himself for his anger problem, but much as he tried to contain his fury, he was unsuccessful. There wasn't even always a valid justification for his outbursts, but whenever Yerachmiel tried to stay calm, he would descend into a deep sadness. He would find himself sinking into a black and bottomless pit whose slimy walls were coated with awfully painful feelings of abandonment and worthlessness. All the skeletons of his youth would come back to haunt and taunt him mercilessly. The slightest slight, true or perceived, was enough to reawaken in Yerachmiel those old feelings of abandonment and worthlessness. His fury helped him fill up that pit and bring him back up to ground level. There was no way he would give it up!

TORAH LESSON

After Hashem informed Moshe of the *eigel*, He asked of Moshe: "And now let go of Me and My anger shall flare up in them and I shall annihilate them."[30] Why did Hashem want to get angry; wouldn't it be more in line with Hashem's attributes of mercy to allow the anger to dissipate?

The Ohr HaChaim explains that when one is deeply hurt by another, he could react in one of two ways. He could either become furious and seek revenge, or he could calm down via consolation and solace.

Hashem, the very source of kindness and compassion constantly allows for reconciliation. However, this time was different. Hashem told Moshe that the offense of Bnei Yisrael's infidelity was so great and the insult so deep that no amount of consolation would be sufficient. Thus, the only option would be to allow for the fury to boil up and to annihilate the entire nation. However, Hashem didn't want to hurt Moshe so He consoled Moshe by promising to turn his descendants into a great nation.

Moshe didn't accept Hashem's consolation, and he literally became sick over the impending annihilation of the Klal Yisrael. Additionally, Moshe worked very hard to rekindle the love of Hashem for Bnei Yisrael. Moshe told Hashem that Bnei Yisrael were His nation and their obliteration would be His loss. He spoke of how it was through them that

---

30   *Shemos* 32:10.

Hashem's greatness became known in the world. Moshe also brought up the merit of the Patriarchs. Additionally, Moshe claimed that killing Bnei Yisrael would result in a tremendous *chillul Hashem*.

Moshe offered so many comforting arguments that Hashem allowed Himself to be consoled even for the previously inconsolable pain.

LIFE LESSON

What is so exciting about anger?

Who says it's so exciting? Well, there obviously must be something very gratifying about allowing oneself to fly off the handle. Why else would otherwise respectable people make a total laughingstock of themselves by blowing steam like an antiquated steam engine?

We know full well that anger and temper outbursts are considered taboo and are viewed as a complete lack of self-control. Angry people are ridiculed and referred to anger management groups. So why do we still get angry? We're successful at overcoming many childlike behaviors — why is anger an exception? What is it that turns foul-tasting anger into something sweet smelling and enticing?

Well, truth be told, anger is very useful for us and it would simply be a shame to dispose of something so valuable. Sounds strange, doesn't it? After all, besides for volcanologists, who enjoys volcanoes? It inflicts so much damage; what could be good about it? Let's head out on an educational, fact finding discovery trip to the heart of the volcano (or is it the volcano of the heart?).

When we've been cheated or short-handed, we tend to feel used and manipulated. This causes us to feel foolish and gullible. Our egos take a serious beating. This sudden shrinking of our egos creates a void within us, which gets flooded with feelings of distress and misery and throws us off balance. We then feel a strong urge to fill the void in order to regain our balance and self-respect. Such massive inner tremors of the tectonic plates are surely enough to set off a volcano!

We allow ourselves to get washed over with tidal waves of anger and a powerful desire for revenge. The anger causes our bodies to produce lots of energy, which in turn fills our beings with physical energy and a sense of empowerment. It helps plug the holes in our egos and lifts us from our distress. This angry energy then propels us to take revenge, which we hope will restore our sense of balance. The world will feel just once again.

So anger surely is valuable, isn't it?

Well, there is no arguing with success. However, taking into consideration the many side effects, it may be worthwhile to find alternative methods of treatment.

A second approach to heal a cheated ego is via reconciliation and compensation. Hurt feelings can be treated by the potent salve of compensation and an abundance of positive and good feelings. Reconciliation is very powerful and can bring a relationship to new heights. Appeasement and reconciliation are like a balm to one's wounded ego and can help it heal in a healthy way. The void that was created by the pain can be filled with positive emotions of forgiveness, providing the person with a new sense of wholesomeness.

While the first method of dealing with anger comes more easily and is simpler to implement, it leaves destruction and even more pain in its wake.

The second approach might take more effort and willpower, but those who are brave enough to try it claim that it is well worth it.

Anger could be useful, but reconciliation is always more beneficial!

WE TEACH PEOPLE HOW TO TREAT US

S hmuel felt like a pushover. He knew he was worthless and didn't deserve to have a good life. His boss was quick to pick up on Shmuel's attitude and maximize its potential. He made Shmuel work at the most unfavorable hours for minimal compensation — and Shmuel never complained. At the home front, things weren't too good either. His wife and kids treated him as no more than an undesirable piece of furniture. His siblings and siblings-in-law treated him with total disregard. Shmuel never complained and never stood up for his rights, for in his eyes he had no rights.

Shmuel viewed this world as a long and dark tunnel, enveloped in a thick and palpable darkness that didn't allow any light to shine through. He had no hopes of ever reaching the light at the end of the tunnel. He couldn't even imagine there was any light there, at least not for him. The only light he could envision was situated way past the gloomy tunnel called life.

Then, Shmuel started ever so reluctantly to explore the possibility that maybe he was worth at least something. He started projecting more self-worth and sticking up for his rights. He was amazed at how quickly people learned to treat him differently. The more Shmuel changed, the more the people around him changed their way of interacting with him. He even overheard his boss tell some friends that "Shmuel is a different person."

Shmuel had discovered the switch to turn on the light in his dark tunnel.

TORAH LESSON

The Torah tells us how following the abduction of Dina by Shechem, the sons of Yaakov massacred the entire city. Following the massacre, Hashem instructed Yaakov to go to Beis El to fulfill his vow and build a *mizbei'ach*. The Torah relates, "And they traveled and the fear of Hashem was upon the cities that were around them and they didn't chase after the sons of Yaakov."[31]

The Ohr HaChaim explains that the Torah is telling us that is was an amazing miracle that Yaakov was able to travel in peace. It's quite possible that the neighboring nations were originally afraid of Yaakov's sons. However, Yaakov's departure from the environs of Shechem should have naturally been interpreted as a cowardly move, as a sign of fear of retaliation. Human nature dictates that a show of fear greatly increases the chances of being attacked. Thus, the escape should have provoked the nations to chase after Yaakov. And yet, Yaakov amazingly traveled in peace.

Thus, we see that it's part of human nature to take the cue from the people themselves how to treat them.

---

31   *Bereishis* 35:5.

LIFE LESSON

Life is a perplexing mystery, isn't it?

Why are some treated with love and respect while others are ridiculed and derided? Why do some stroll down the avenue of life surrounded by many doting friends, while others drag their feet as they trudge down the lonely path of life?

In fact, we could make an argument that life really is a mystery on many fronts and perplexing in many ways. There are many aspects of our lives beyond our ability to change and where we have no input.

However, with regards to the way others treat us, not only do we have input, we're actually the ones holding the keys! We ourselves serve as the guides to the perplexed and teach others how to treat us. Enlightening, isn't it?

Or rather, it's enlightening and frightening simultaneously! How is that?

The recognition that we ourselves wield the power to decide how people will treat us is good news and bad news.

The good news is that when we dislike the way we're being treated we need not despair; we can change it.

The bad news is that so long as we don't change it ourselves, the situation will remain very much unchanged. So let's remain positive and focus on the good news!

How are we in control of the way others behave toward us? It's quite simple: our behaviors cue people how to treat us. They observe how we interact with and treat others. Even more importantly, they scrutinize how we treat ourselves! The way we carry ourselves, the way we speak, and the way we behave all send messages of how we expect to be treated.

More still, the way others treat us could serve as a barometer to measure our treatment of others and ourselves and of our general behavior. If we get the feeling that we're constantly being stepped on, it might just be that we're giving off an impression of being a doormat. If we find others avoiding us, perhaps we appear in their eyes as an angry bull, which is best avoided. Thus, by reflecting on the way others treat us, we can get a pretty clear picture of the image we're projecting.

However, we need not agonize over the way we've been treated thus far. We have the ability to change that and to improve the way others will be treating us from here on. It's very simple. We just have to work on implementing change on our end and most people will learn to dance to our new beat.

In the event we see others are avoiding us and we realize that it's due to our anger, we could start by subduing the angry bull. We could start treating others the way we would like to be treated. Chances are, once they realize that the danger has passed, they will start interacting with us in a much more positive way.

The same holds true with the doormat phenomenon. We need only decide to abandon our position on the floor next to the door. So long as we were lying on the floor, the people standing around us found it inconvenient to bend down to interact with us as equals. However, once we stand up and are face to face with the others, they'll find it much easier to treat us as equals! Additionally, as the laws of physics dictate, when we're standing upright it's very inconvenient for other people to step on us.

The world is our mirror. It reflects back to us the image we project!

THOU SHALT NOT HAVE OTHER GODS

Shimon was "the" man. He knew how to balance his numerous responsibilities yet still come across as a calm and patient person. He was busy with his flourishing business, involved in many communal activities, and he managed to learn a few hours a day. He always had time for everyone and was never frazzled by anything. And even with everything going on, Shimon was always punctual and could always be counted on. How some people envied him! Shimon was viewed by many as a role-model. They could see only positive in him; he seemed almost free of all negative traits or human shortcomings.

Shimon was undeniably an impressive person. What people didn't know about was the inner mess and emotional turmoil that was Shimon's lot. Self-doubt gnawed incessantly at his innards. Shimon was terrified that if any of his human weaknesses were to leak out, people would no longer like him and he'd be deemed worthless. He worked very hard to cover up those weaknesses and to portray an image of perfection for all to envy. As a result, Shimon suffered constantly from migraines, anxiety, and panic. Yet Shimon refused to let go because he viewed the consequences as but a small tax to pay in order to feel worthwhile.

TORAH LESSON

Hashem sent Moshe to surprise Pharaoh at his early morning session at the Nile. Why indeed did Pharaoh go daily unescorted to the Nile? And what was so special about Pharaoh's going to the water that Hashem made it a point to specifically send Moshe to meet him there?

The Ohr HaChaim explains it with a Midrash.[32] The Midrash says that Pharaoh fancied himself a god and therefore pretended to be free of any typical physical needs.[33] In order to cover up his humanity and appear super-human, Pharaoh refrained from answering any call of nature the entire day. He made it a routine to sneak out early every morning and relieve himself at the Nile. It must have been torturous, but Pharaoh put up with it with godly perseverance. Hashem wanted Pharaoh to realize that his charade was over. There was no point in him pretending that he was above and beyond the shortcomings of any other mortal.

LIFE LESSON

Who still worships petty gods?

It's quite possible that we ourselves do! Some of us have a tendency to worship ourselves with godly reverence. We feel a need to portray an image of ourselves as perfect beings. We work very hard to cover up our shortcomings, and we feel inferior and ashamed when they're exposed. Now, we're well aware that "human" and "shortcoming" are basically

---

32 *Shemos* 7:16.
33 *Shemos Rabbah* 8:3.

synonymous. And yet, we try to represent ourselves with godly perfection. We're afraid. What will other people think of us if they realize that we are merely flawed humans? They'd surely recoil at the very thought of associating with such "lowly people" and we would be left isolated. Wouldn't we?

It's funny that while we're trying to cover up our own imperfections, we're very much aware that others have shortcomings too. We call their bluff and know that they're not perfect gods. But, we still convince ourselves that they'd only be accepting of us if we were to be perfect. We continue to extend great effort to ensure that no one will recognize our shortcomings, but, understandably, we too are unsuccessful in really fooling anyone.

So, we're in this charade together; we're aware of each other's weaknesses even as we each continue to perfect our cover-up. It's not even like we really end up fooling anyone; they see through our cover-up pretty much the same way we see through theirs! Worse still, no one even cares whether we're perfect or not. In fact, they desperately hope for our performance not to be all that great because they need to outperform us in order for them to feel worthwhile. They might be using us as their barometer to measure their own performance. Hence, they'd possibly be much happier to see us as the imperfect humans that we are.

What a bunch of nonsense!

We invest endless resources only to accomplish the opposite of what we set out to accomplish. We might even know it and yet we still continue to do it! Instead of living and enjoying life, we're wasting our time in drama school learning how to better play god. What a waste of time!

Let's step out of the pantheon. Let's remember that planet earth was designated as the habitat for the simple earthling humans. As such, flawed humans stand a much better chance of feeling comfortable down here. Deities will always feel anxious and out of place among humans on planet Earth. We ought to proudly embrace our flaws; it's our rite of passage into the exclusive humanity club! One of the greatest bonuses of club membership is the ability to access the serenity lounge.

Additionally, let's just imagine how boring life would be if we were all perfect and flawless.

The weird part is that once we become comfortable with our own shortcomings, we'll find that others also feel more comfortable around us. Being open about our shortcomings will allow for our natural selves to emerge, and it will allow those around us to also behave more naturally. We know that natural tastes much better than artificial. Yes, humans are actually worth more when they're flawed!

It's our imperfections that make us perfect human beings!

YOU ARE NOT A
VICTIM OF DESTINY!

Baruch had every justification for slacking off in yeshiva and for honing his internet addiction. His father had passed away when Baruch was still a baby, and his stepfather was strange and detached; there was no love lost between them.

The situation with his mother was not much better. They would often lock horns and their arguments would grow loud and fierce. The arguments would usually end in his mother accusing Baruch of ruining her marriage. In fact, Baruch did indeed try very hard to do just that. When things would get out of control, his mother would threaten to call the police on him.

As for his siblings, they were much older than Baruch and they each had their own families. They felt deep shame from the state of affairs in their mother's home and they tried to steer clear of it.

Baruch felt contempt towards his mother and alienation towards his siblings. He was alone in the world and felt that no one truly loved him or cared for him. It didn't help matters that at age twenty-seven, Baruch was among the older group in his yeshiva and had no friends.

It was not his fault, he claimed, that destiny had dealt him such a tough one. Baruch saw no reason to refrain from indulging in internet use. Being online became his lifeline. He had no strength to fight destiny so he went along with it.

However, with all his justifications, Baruch still felt miserable. The internet and gadgetry didn't fill his needs. Over time, Baruch learned to disregard his excuses and to get in touch with his true inner self. He discovered that he could use his challenges as a means to strengthen his character and become a more sensitive and understanding person — definitely an asset in married life.

TORAH LESSON

The Gemara states: "Whoever was born in the *mazal* of *Ma'adim* will shed blood. Said Rabbi Ashi, (he could be) a blood-letter, a bandit, a *shochet*, or a *mohel*."[34]

The Ohr HaChaim uses this Gemara to explain the *pasuk*, "*Im b'chukosai teileichu v'es mitzvosai tishmoru*."[35] The positioning of the planets during birth can have a strong influence on the formation of one's nature and temperament.

What's the point then in trying to improve one's personality traits? If one were born in the *mazal* of *Ma'adim* he'll grow into a brigand and murderer. What's the point in trying to fight destiny? Furthermore, we

---

34   *Shabbos* 156a.
35   *Vayikra* 26:3.

shouldn't even be held accountable for our actions; they were predestined. We're not at fault!

Thus, the Torah is telling us that even if the laws of nature (the *mazalos*) have bestowed upon us certain qualities and urges, all is not over. Our fate has not been sealed. The urge to shed blood can be realized in its basest form as murder, it can be channeled into a means of income as a professional blood-letter, or it can be utilized for a mitzvah by becoming a ritual slaughterer or a *mohel*. One absolutely has free choice to answer his calling in whichever way he chooses. We are fully accountable.

LIFE LESSON

Why does destiny seem so unfair sometimes? Why do we repeatedly encounter blockages in life?

Well, honestly, we don't know!

We have absolutely no idea why we've been given certain challenges. Of course we could try and crack the mystery by delving deeply into our painful history. We could spend as much time as we please every single day reviewing our bad luck. We could analyze every single hardship that we have had to face. If it makes us feel good, let's go for it.

What for? Why should we sit and lament our hardships? We'd just be wasting precious time that we could utilize for forging ahead. So long as we're focused on the blockages, we won't be able to concentrate on finding ways to circumvent them!

How can we find ways to circumvent these blockages and what will we accomplish by doing that?

Before we plunge into it, let's clear our minds by taking a stroll along the riverbank.

As the water flows, it encounters many obstacles in its course. There are boulders, huge mountains, insurmountable blockages, and sudden drops. Should the water stop flowing and stay put, it'll turn stagnant and become a breeding ground for a host of harmful microbes. However, as the water labors to cut through mountains and plunge over cliffs it produces spectacular creations. It creates magnificent canyons, splendid falls, fearsome whirlpools, and frothy rapids. Not only has it not become stagnant, it has by far surpassed the serene majesty of a tranquil river. It has become a drawing point and an inspiration to multitudes!

Now, let's take a walk along the riverbank of life. In the flow of life we are sure to encounter many obstacles — some of us more than others. We could raise our hands in despair and blame it on destiny. After all, there is no denying the existence of those blockages, and some loom quite huge and insurmountable. But we'd be doing ourselves the greatest disservice since we'll just turn stagnant. We'd be providing an opportune breeding ground to anything and everything that's harmful to us.

However, we can also decide to apply ourselves and find ways around or through the challenges. Not only will we be able to continue on our way, we'll be creating something spectacular in the process! We'll be turning those stumbling blocks into stepping stones. We'll be able to use the insight and fortitude that we gained from overcoming the hardships and apply them to other areas in life and help out others in similar trying situations. We might even serve as an inspiration to others facing similar challenges.

All's fine and well, but one can't fight destiny.

How true! One can't fight destiny because it hasn't been created yet! We ourselves create our destiny as we map out the course of our life. True, we're faced with challenging situations that we don't necessarily have control over. But we do have full control over how we'll deal with them!

We're not shaped by destiny. Rather, we shape our destiny!

MARRIAGE
EMPOWERMENT

DON'T CLOSE THAT VENT!

R abbi M. was a true wet-behind-the-ears *rebbi* with practically no experience but loads of enthusiasm. He viewed his ninth-graders — all of them having fallen through the cracks of the typical yeshiva setting — as full of raw potential. He was determined to make a real difference in their lives. In one of his first steps as a *rebbi*, Rabbi M. reached out and connected with the parents. He tried to form a working relationship with them for the benefit of his dear students.

All seemed to be going well, even better than he'd expected. Some parents even expressed their appreciation at his thoughtfulness, and connections were formed. However, when Rabbi M. reached out to Mrs. G., he had second thoughts about this whole idea. As soon as he introduced himself as Yossi's *rebbi*, Mrs. G. let go a whole litany of complaints about her son. For half an hour she just carried on about all the issues she was having with her Yossi.

The young *rebbi* was caught unawares. He had no idea what he was supposed to say or do. One thing he was sure about though was that he had to do whatever was in his power to help this distraught mother and son. Over the next two days, Rabbi M. consulted with some veterans on the *chinuch* scene and worked out a great plan to help improve the situation between Yossi and his mother. He excitedly called Mrs. G. and shared his plan. She thanked him politely for his time and effort.

Rabbi M. eagerly waited to hear how the plan was working — and hear he did. One day the principal mentioned to him, ever so casually, that Mrs. G. had called him, full of indignation at the audacity of this *rebbi* to mix into her private family issues and dictate to her how to live. The principal then advised Rabbi M. never to offer advice unless explicitly asked.

It was a lesson the young *rebbi* would long remember!

TORAH LESSON

Following the incident with Sarah, Avimelech, King of Pelishtim, was full of righteous indignation at Avraham and asked him, "What did we do to you and how did we sin to you that you wrought upon me and my kingdom such a great sin; acts that are not done you did to me." [36] Then Avimelech asked Avraham again, "What did you see that you did such a thing?" Why did Avimelech repeat his question twice, merely changing the phraseology the second time around?

The Ohr HaChaim explains that this was no repetition. The first time Avimelech wasn't questioning Avraham and he wasn't expecting an answer. He was just venting and expressing his hurt at what had transpired. The second time, however, he did question Avraham and expected an answer. And indeed, Avraham's answer only addressed Avimelech's second question, whereas the venting part was left unanswered.

LIFE LESSON

We like to vent, don't we?

We all face many situations that could leave us feeling upset and frustrated. We sometimes feel like boiling steam is rising inside of us; we feel like we're on the verge of a full-blown volcanic explosion. We desperately try to stay in control as we'd rather not be perceived as an active and dangerous volcano. However, it calls for herculean effort to keep cool when there's this steam inside us, since it needs to be released. So we decide to vent to someone close to us, someone we feel comfortable enough sharing our frustration with.

Once we start venting, our suppressed and accumulated steam easily comes spewing out. Out come our frustrations, anger, resentment, guilt, etc. When we're done, we usually feel much better just from releasing all these noxious wastes from our bodies. We're ready to thank the person for listening and move on.

But, wait! Not so fast! We're suddenly faced with this massive deluge of unsolicited advice. Not only did we not ask for it — we don't want it! We just needed someone to express our frustrations to. We definitely weren't interested in lengthy sermons or unwelcome advice. More still, it sometimes makes us feel invalidated, misunderstood, and even violated. We've exposed our weakest spots, but that doesn't mean that we want anyone to enter! When we're lectured, we sometimes end up feeling trampled upon.

So many of us have had such experiences, haven't we?

It would thus stand to reason that we would be extra careful not to make a similar mistake when someone else vents to us.

And, yet, can't we too plead guilty for this very crime? When our spouse vents to us, s/he's not looking for lengthy treatises on the "Theory of Human Adaptability and Adjustability." S/he might be expecting it, but s/he surely doesn't want it! The one venting isn't looking for solutions, at least not right now. All s/he wants is a safe place to kvetch, a devoted spouse who will understand and empathize, nothing more.

In fact, when our spouse vents to us, it's really a compliment in disguise. It's a confirmation that they trust us and feel secure enough to expose their weak spots. Let's withstand our urge to play teacher; let's not lecture or call them to task for their weaknesses. That would only serve to show our spouse that we're totally tuned out to their feelings and we don't even care to try to understand them.

Instead, let's see it for what it is. It's an excellent opportunity to enhance our relationship even more. We can listen and empathize with their hardships. The best support we could offer our spouse is to empathize with them and just to be there for them, to offer them an unclogged listening ear and a steady shoulder to lean on and cry upon, and an open heart to accept them. This will help them feel understood and validated.

As for solutions to the problems at hand, once the vent has cleared up, the one venting will very often come up with workable solutions on their own, without our dispensing our wisdom. Even problems that can't easily be solved tend to feel much lighter once vented.

True empathy is one of the greatest gifts we can offer our spouse.

I — AND ONLY I — AM RIGHT!

The city was covered in a thick blanket of snow. The mercury had again dropped close to zero. Inside the G. home, the heating was working full-force, yet the air still felt frigid. Husband and wife had again gotten into one of their notorious arguments. The temperature continued to drop as the voices persistently rose. The kids tried desperately to get out of the way and disappear. They felt terrified and confused watching the horrific argument between father and mother.

Mr. and Mrs. G. didn't even know how they got to this point. They'd started out married life much the idyllic couple as anyone else. They'd shared hopes and dreams of building a home filled with peace and love, but theirs was anything but. The dream of peace lay shattered in pieces in some forgotten corner and the hope of love was hopelessly dropped as soon as the arguments started.

They found themselves constantly locking horns over wife's spending habits. Husband would accuse wife of wasting all their money on unnecessary frivolities and wife argued that husband was being overly stingy. She claimed that the expenses were necessary in order to keep up a certain standard and image. Beneath the façade of anger there was a strong feeling of raw pain as both husband and wife felt invalidated and misunderstood.

TORAH LESSON

The Torah states, "And the fifteenth day of this month [Nissan] shall be a festival of matzos to Hashem."[37] Chazal deduct from this verse that only on Pesach is matzah eaten, whereas on Succos matzah is not eaten even though Succos appears, by the act of moving into a succah, to be a greater celebration of our leaving Egypt.[38] Chazal also deduct from a different *pasuk* that there is no mitzvah to build a succah on Pesach — even though it would seem like a greater celebration of our leaving Egypt — due to the commandment to eat only matzah.[39]

The *Mishneh L'Melech* is bothered by these two Chazals.[40] If one understands that Succos is greater than Pesach and we therefore need a *pasuk* to tell us not to eat matzah on Succos, how can one then make a turnaround and claim that Pesach is greater? And why then do we need an additional *pasuk* to tell us that we need not build a succah on Pesach?

The Ohr HaChaim explains that in truth, both arguments have equal merit.[41] While one scholar might think in one direction, another scholar might think in the opposite direction. Thus, the Torah paid heed to both arguments.

37   *Vayikra* 23:6.
38   *Toras Kohanim*, Chapter 11.
39   Ibid., Chapter 14.
40   *Hilchos Chametz Umatzah* 6:1.
41   *Vayikra* 14:7.

We are well aware of how precise and accounted for every letter in the Torah is. And yet the Torah deemed it necessary to address every possible perspective. We can see from this that there is a possibility of more than one valid opinion.

LIFE LESSON

What is as much a part of married life as living under one roof? Differences of opinion, of course!

It's one of the mysteries of creation, but it's an established law in physics. Place two people in one room and there will be differences of opinion. There is simply no getting around this law; it's as old as the world itself! Yes, we'll surely have differences of opinion with our spouse.

We might claim that we have no problem with that. We believe that we can tolerate a difference of opinion and we can disagree like adults. But we don't reach that stage all that often. In the heat of a disagreement it's easy to convince ourselves that our spouse's opinion simply makes no sense! If we're open-minded, there's got to be an opinion to be open-minded about. We're not just going to accept nonsense! So, we lovingly try to prove to our spouse that their opinion made no sense. We feel driven by our love and sense of spousal duty to enlighten our significant other of their irrationality.

Much as we might be convinced that we're just trying to convince our spouse of their irrationality, they may not see it that way. Instead, they could interpret it as our inability to tolerate another opinion. The topic at hand then becomes irrelevant as the disagreement takes a personal turn. Fighting is not our style and we have no intention to go there. We only want our spouse to see where their childish behavior has taken us.

If only we could disagree like adults that would be fine. The problem is simply that our spouse has no idea how to do that! Or is it really only about him/her? Did we even try to listen to our spouse to see if s/he actually had a point?

We have this funny preconceived notion that disagreements can only go in one direction — win-lose; if we are right, then our spouse is obviously wrong. And worse still, if we give merit to our spouse, we're declaring ourselves as wrong.

In truth, we could have disagreements without the need to be the only one who's right. We could learn to employ the win-win formula. I can have a valid point and so can my spouse. Validating our spouse doesn't necessarily invalidate ourselves.

How is that so? Well, if we'd think about it, we'd realize that arguments are seldom about dry facts — they're usually about perceptions. Now, a difference in perception is much more tolerable than disagreeing about the actual facts. Once we acknowledge that there can be more than one perspective, we can tolerate more than one opinion.

There is, however, one precondition to properly implementing this new win-win strategy. We need to feel secure and confident with ourselves. Otherwise, every argument and disagreement will turn into a self-worth test, a challenge to our very being. With such high stakes, who can risk losing? Thus, we understandably become obsessed with winning.

Thinking and arguing with a win-win mindset can take some effort but it's surely worth it. Our spouses will appreciate that we understand them, and they in turn will be more open to understanding us. So here's the paradox: we stand a much better chance of getting our way by acknowledging our spouse's way!

Here's a bonus benefit to following the win-win model: it'll fill our hearts with feelings of happiness and serenity, and it'll give us confidence. Who would forgo that?

Losers have a need to always win; true winners can afford to allow another person to win!

THE FLIMSINESS OF FACADES

Yitzi was the pride of his parents. They bragged about him nonstop to whoever cared to listen, and even to those who didn't. He had himself tested on many hundreds of *blatt* Gemara! He was a gem of a boy, a *nachas* role-model. Yitzi had worked long and hard to reach the peak; once there, he continued working to maintain his status. This new status felt so good and so right. People looked up to him and he looked up to himself. He was no commoner; he was a boy of status. His opinions mattered and others wanted to be considered his friend. True there was a more restrictive code of conduct that went along with this status, but it was well worth it!

Yitzi married the daughter of a prestigious *rosh yeshiva*. The *shidduch* was a no-brainer; everyone knew that Yitzi was destined to become a *rosh yeshiva*. And they lived happily ever after.

Actually, no they didn't.

Yitzi was always tense, moody, and withdrawn. He wasn't really there for his wife and when she voiced her concerns, he just brushed them off. This went on for some time and then the huge tower he had worked so hard to create came crashing down. It became apparent that Yitzi wasn't up to much. With a huff and a puff, gone was the *masmid*, gone was the future *rosh yeshiva*, gone was his father's pride.

TORAH LESSON

The Gemara relates: Shimon HaTzaddik said, "I never ate from the *korban* of a *nazir* who became impure, but for once.[42] An exceptionally handsome *nazir*, with pretty eyes and gorgeous locks, made his appearance in the Beis Hamikdash. I asked him, 'My son, what prompted you to [take on the *nezirus* and, thus] ruin your beautiful hair?' He responded, 'Once, I saw my reflection in the water and my evil inclination started burning within me and it wanted to eliminate me from the world. I then vowed that I will cut my hair for Hashem's sake.' At once, I stood up and I kissed him on his head. I said to him, 'My son, may there be more people like you in Israel.'"

The Ohr HaChaim uses this Gemara to explain the repetition of the word *nazir* in the *pasuk*, "*Lindor neder, nazir l'hazir laHashem.*"[43] He says the first *nazir* refers to the one who takes upon himself the vow of *nezirus* for various external reasons. This one is not *laHashem*, for Hashem's sake, whereas the second one is a *nazir* purely for Hashem's sake. He is thus on a much higher level.

So we see two identical *nezirim* who appear alike outwardly, yet one was praised by Shimon HaTzaddik while the other one was despised.

---

42   *Nedarim* 9b.
43   *Bamidbar* 6:2.

How were they different? Simple. One had Hashem in mind and he really meant it, while the other one did it for some ulterior motive.

LIFE LESSON

Are we for real?

Well, let's think about it. Is there perhaps a possibility that we demand certain behaviors or impose limitations on ourselves and our spouse that we don't really believe in? Are there times when we do things not out of true conviction, but in order to create or maintain a certain image of ourselves? We ought to question our actions and determine how much of what we do is really just some kind of act.

It's quite possible that there was something in our childhood or adolescence that caused us to believe that being our real selves would hinder our success in life. We felt the need to recreate ourselves. So we went ahead and diligently erected an elaborate and impressive façade.

When we were in *shidduchim*, we convinced ourselves that people saw only our impersonation and that's why we were able to get a decent *shidduch*. Our spouse got to know and appreciate that other person, while we were careful to keep our real selves out of sight. By now, we feel that even if we wanted to, there is obviously no way we could suddenly bring our true selves into our married life. It'll surely be an unwelcome intrusion!

Now, while our phony edifice may look impressive, it usually has none of the basic amenities. We were so busy tending the façade that we had no time to care about the rest of the structure. Thus, we often feel stiflingly repressed and live in constant fear of the building collapsing.

While we're great and proud on the outside, we're cowering in fear on the inside! We might believe that in reality we're not good enough and that we are unlikeable. We're terrified of exposing our true selves and facing possible rejection.

Perhaps we feel safer maintaining two identities, but is it fair to our spouse to keep in our home another person s/he's not aware of? If we believe that our marriage is due to our impersonation, do we care enough about our marriage? Or are we too preoccupied with maintaining our façade?

If and when our façades crumble, as they tend to, what will be left of us? The true picture will then reveal itself and there will be nowhere to hide. We'll have no personality and no true family life! So why should we keep on investing in something that will come back to haunt us?

Let's remember that the calculations we made years ago might be outdated. Let's look at it from an adult perspective and reevaluate our priorities. Let's remember that we owe it to ourselves and to our spouse to be our true selves. Let's come out of that dark and stifling place for some sunlight and fresh air. In the brightness of the sunlight we'll be able to get a better look at ourselves. We might be pleasantly surprised at what we see.

Chances are, your true self is much better than you give it credit for. Even if there are things we need to correct, once we remove the façade we'll be able to invest our efforts and our resources in becoming a truer self and truer spouse. We'll then be able to go on and build a solid marriage on solid ground. It might not be such a glitzy façade, but it will be a solid and valuable structure! We owe it to ourselves and our spouses!

---

*A simple and solid building is much more valuable
than an elaborate façade!*

THE HAZINESS OF HASTE

Thereﾠwas no getting around them. Day after day, David had to rough various challenges that wore away at his patience and composure. As a result, at the end of each day David would generally very snappy. His challenges went something like this:

- His boss would send some mean comments his way.
- The sandwich he'd bought for lunch would be spoiled.
- Traffic on the way home would move at a snail's pace.
- He'd have to circle the block five times in search of a parking spot, and then have to settle for one far away.

Very often, he was faced with more than one of these challenges on the same day.

On this particular day, David had a bonus aggravation. As he stepped out of his car, he tripped and fell right into a muddy puddle.

By the time David reached his front door, he had a smashing headache, frayed nerves, an injured ego, a rumbling stomach, bruised hands, and a muddied suit. David hoped for some peaceful quiet and a hot nourishing dinner, but he was in for a disappointment.

His wife, as is the case with all mothers, had also been dealt a slew of challenges that day:

- A child refused to go to school and the pleading and convincing totally drained her.
- The baby woke up with a fever and was super cranky.
- She waited in the doctor's office for a very long time, trying unsuccessfully to soothe the baby.
- Despite everything, she still worked hard to get a tasty and nourishing supper ready on time, but then had to deal with the kids' negative comments about the food.

On that fateful day, wife had impatiently awaited David's arrival in order to share with him the details of her day. When he finally showed up an hour late, he was greeted with, "Where have you been? Why didn't you tell me you'd be late? Now the supper is cold! And I have no time to talk to you."

It was more than David could handle at the moment. He responded with a sharp retort, which was followed by an animated shouting match. The saga ended with wife retreating to the bedroom and David storming out of the house. It took them a long time to repair the damage inflicted on their marriage by their hasty behaviors.

TORAH LESSON

The Gemara[44] infers from the *pasuk* that if someone in Eretz Yisrael sells his field, he may not buy it back before two years.[45] The Ohr HaChaim asks why did the Torah prohibit the purchaser from reselling the land to its original owner? Why should this be different than any other monetary matter, where a person has the freedom to do with his possessions as he pleases?

The Ohr HaChaim explains that the Torah generally looks askance at a person selling his ancestral estate. However, at times, one might find himself in dire straits and he'll hastily sell his field. Therefore, the Torah, in its infinite wisdom, placed this repurchasing restriction on the seller. This restriction will hopefully cause the seller to rethink his initial idea and back away from the deal before it starts.

It's possible that besides for the actual fear of the restriction, which might cause the seller to retract, there might be an additional factor at work here. A person in dire straits tends to make hasty decisions, which he is bound to regret later on. The time gained by pausing before jumping into the sale might be just enough for his rational thinking to kick in, and it's quite possible he'll decide to back off.

LIFE LESSON

I should have!

I shouldn't have!

Why did I do it?

Why didn't I do it?

Does this sound familiar?

Regret — it's very familiar to us! We spend enough time in the company of regret that we've come to see it as an old, albeit pesky, friend.

Is it normal to rethink our actions? Absolutely! Is our regret unfounded? Not necessarily!

---

44   *Arachin* 29b.
45   *Vayikra* 25:15.

We work so hard all day. We try to work on restraining our impulses and carefully choosing our words and actions. This impulse control calls for lots of inner strength and could deplete us of our energy. By the time the day is over, we're very often running on low and that's how we get home.

We're edgy and irritable and we have little strength left to restrain our impulsivity. After especially tough days, we are almost like fireworks just waiting for a spark to ignite us. When that spark comes, we put on some impressive show. Suddenly, those word matches, temper tantrums, silent treatments, door banging, and the like that we'd thought we'd graduated from in grade school are the vogue again.

Maybe it felt good venting our frustration by being impulsive. We might have enjoyed the nostalgia of revisiting kindergarten, but the regret and repercussions — there's nothing nostalgic about that! Those comments we made and the way we behaved in the haze of our haste have a tendency to come back and haunt us for a long time. They could bear painful and long-lasting consequences. Once the damage is done, it's very hard to reverse it. Regret is definitely in place in some situations. However, regret isn't necessarily very useful and is best when used in moderation. So let's keep our reasons for regret to a minimum. Let's pay attention to the Torah's lesson and refrain from being hasty reactionaries. There really is no point in revisiting kindergarten; there are new preschoolers filling those small chairs and our intrusion is uncalled for. We're much more appreciated when we fill our adult roles!

But can't we ever just be natural and let down our guard, especially at home? And the answer is yes, of course we could — and should — be natural! Natural adults, that is.

Our spouses chose us with the belief that we're adults; we owe it to them to prove them right. Let's practice refraining from reacting in the heat of the moment. We can work on making it a habit to interact with our spouse only in a cool and controlled way.

As soon as we feel the heat within us rising, we should know that it's time to cool down. We can have some cooldown practices on the ready.

It could be stepping out for a few minutes or engaging in a fun activity. When we feel we're about to lose control, we can calmly and sincerely tell our spouse that we're not in the right frame of mind to discuss this topic just now — we're afraid we'll say or do the wrong thing. This will help us stay in control of our impulses. Once we feel up to it, we could broach the subject in a calm and respectful way.

Things done in haste will leave us with a bad taste!

FORGIVENESS VS. REPRESSION

The Grosses started out much like many newlywed couples. At first they were in the clouds, and then they were in the dumps. There was so much misunderstanding, so many times Mrs. Gross felt hurt by her husband's actions or words.

She knew bearing grudges wasn't good for her marriage so after every incident she would try to forgive her husband. But for some reason, she kept remembering those incidents and made sure to occasionally remind her husband of them. Mr. Gross couldn't understand; he'd asked her so many times for forgiveness and she said she'd forgiven him! Additionally, what about the many times she'd wronged him and he'd forgiven her — couldn't she reciprocate?

Eventually, there was so much resentment and so much suppressed anger that they weren't even interested in making it work anymore. They had "forgiven" each other too many times and now they just wanted out. They were miserable over the prospect of divorce, but they were even more miserable at the thought of staying together.

TORAH LESSON

Moshe Rabbeinu served Bnei Yisrael in the most devoted way possible. Time and again, he placed himself in the line of fire, risking and sometimes incurring Hashem's wrath while beseeching Him for the sake of Bnei Yisrael. There wasn't a thing the devoted shepherd Moshe didn't do for his flock. And what did he receive in return? He forfeited his lifelong dream of entering Eretz Yisrael!

There are various explanations as to why Moshe was barred from entering Eretz Yisrael, and they're all tied with the Bnei Yisrael:

- So he wouldn't build the Beis Hamikdash, which would prevent it from being destroyed, thus forcing Hashem to spill His wrath on the Jews instead of on the Beis Hamikdash.[46]
- So he could bring those who died in the *midbar* to *Olam Habah*.[47]
- To atone for the sin of Pe'or.[48] He would stand guard against the Pe'or whenever it would attempt to refresh the sin of Bnei Yisrael.[49]

However, in no way did this affect Moshe's devotion and love for his people. And more, before his passing, when the painful reality of not being allowed into Eretz Yisrael stared him in the face, Moshe went on to bestow upon them blessings in abundance. It was this

---

46 *Midrash Tehillim*, Chapter 79.
47 *Sifri, Devarim* 33:21.
48 Talmud, *Sotah* 14a.
49 *Pirkei D'Rebbi Eliezer*, Chapter 45.

superhuman display of *middos* that earned Moshe the unmatched title of *Ish ha'Elokim*.[50]

Let's think about it. Moshe spent one hundred and twenty days in *shamayim*, he spoke to Hashem in the closest manner possible, he was the only one to hear all *Aseres Hadibros* directly from Hashem, and the Torah is called *Toras Moshe*. And yet, all these reasons were not enough to earn him this title. It was only his extraordinary dedication to and love for his people, in spite of all that they did to him, that elevated him to such a lofty point.

LIFE LESSON

What's married life all about?

Hey, that's one unfair question!

It's about many things — there are so many details to married life. How is it possible to conceptualize and package it into one sentence?

True, no arguing with that point! Still, let's try to focus on just one very important aspect of married life. Well, not simply an important aspect but a master key to a healthy and stable marriage.

FORGIVENESS.

Now there, no kidding around, we all know about forgiveness; we've all practiced it and we've all asked for it. So what's this big shebang about it? Where's the "key" we were promised? It surely is not this (obvious) forgiveness thing!

Additionally, we've seen many couples who knew all about forgiving each other, yet their marriages ended up derailing! Chances are, we too had plenty of opportunities to forgive our spouses, but not always did it really help to improve our marriages. We might even feel a niggling resentment when we think of how much we've had to forgive. So much for forgiveness!

Truth is, it's unfair for us to judge forgiveness in absentee; chances are we haven't met forgiveness face to face. If we view forgiving as a chore to be done and over with, then we don't even know what

---

50   *Ohr HaChaim, Devarim* 33:1-2.

forgiveness means. That chore is really called repression, not forgive-ness! Repression is an imposter impersonating forgiveness. Repression is not even such a difficult chore: we simply push the hurt away from the forefront and we file it away in the back of our minds.

The filing room is filled with files of all the hurts we've endured from our spouse. Whenever we get bitten by the nostalgia bug, we make a pilgrimage to that filing room and we lose ourselves (and our marriages) in the memories of yesteryear. We become invigorated by the refreshed memories of our own greatness as evidenced by the sheer number of times we forgave our spouse. What a simple way to boost our sense of superiority in marriage. What a simple and easy way to destroy our marriage! Surely no key is needed there!

Forgiveness couldn't be more different from repression. Forgiveness is no chore; it's a beautiful art and an exact science! As with any art, it calls upon us to apply our hearts and feelings to the matter. A half-hearted forgiveness isn't going to fetch a high price — it's worthless! We need to tap into our feelings of love and connection to help us to even want to work on forgiveness.

We can now move on to the science of forgiveness. This part entails understanding that there might just be another side to the story that we're not aware of. It calls for accepting the fact that, much to our chagrin, we've married someone as human as ourselves. We make mistakes and we want forgiveness, and so does our spouse. This synthesis of art and science will help us create a truly unique masterpiece!

But why should we invest so much time and effort in forgiving our spouse? Do they deserve it after what they did?!

Let's not even think about our spouses. Let's think only about our-selves. We surely deserve a happy and enjoyable marriage! True forgive-ness is just a key to get there. Let's make use of this key and enjoy a happy and fulfilling marriage!

As for that storage room, why should we waste precious space? We could renovate this space and turn it into a cozy family room where we could spend quality time with our spouse! Isn't that much more exciting?

The beauty of our marriage is dependent on our mastery of the art of forgiveness!

WHAT DOES YOUR SPOUSE REALLY WANT?

Mrs. G. was very frustrated. She felt her husband didn't care for her and was oblivious to her needs. Mr. G. was frustrated by his wife's complaints. He tried to be so caring of his wife. Whenever an issue arose, he would try to correct it and make sure that his wife had whatever she needed. But no matter how much he tried, Mrs. G. still complained that she felt her needs weren't validated and that her husband just didn't get it. Following is just one example.

Wife complained about the run-ins she kept on having with her *shvigger*. Husband really wanted to help her out so he refrained from siding with his mother. He even went way out of his comfort zone and spoke to his mother about it. He then happily informed his wife that the issue was taken care of. He was sure he'd just proven himself and his wife would appreciate how much he did for her. Instead, wife was mortified and really upset with him. He, in turn, was hurt. He had gone and spoken to his mother even though he felt very uncomfortable doing it. What did he get in return? Never mind the thank you, but why the attitude? It really didn't pay to try and be good to his wife!

What really happened here? His wife had actually hoped he'd offer her some advice on how to prove herself to her mother-in-law. His actions accomplished exactly the opposite. He had totally missed the point!

TORAH LESSON

Rashi quotes a Midrash: "Why is the *parashah* of the menorah juxtaposed with that of the *nesi'im*?[51] Because when Aharon watched the *nesi'im* inaugurate the *mizbei'ach*, he felt slighted that neither he nor his tribe took part in the inauguration. Hashem promised him, 'Yours is greater than theirs, for you will cleanse and light the menorah every day.'"

The Ohr HaChaim wonders: There were so many components to the *avodah* in the *Mishkan*. There were the various *korbanos* and the *ketores* — there was so much the *kohanim* did on a daily basis in the *Mishkan*. Why was it that Hashem consoled Aharon specifically with the cleansing and lighting of the menorah?

He goes on to explain that Aharon was hurt for missing out on the inaugural part. Reassuring him with the *avodah* of the *korbanos* would be missing the point! That was not what Aharon felt that he had missed out on!

The consolation with the menorah, however, was right on target. When the menorah was cleansed, the actual lamps were either removed,

---

51   *Bamidbar* 8:2.

or at least bent downward, cleansed and then rearranged. Thus, it had an aspect of renewal and inauguration daily. This was a fitting compensation for Aharon's missing out on the initial inauguration.

LIFE LESSON

It's our intentions that count, right?

The main thing is that our spouse knows that we really intended to please them, isn't that true? Well, it might be. In many instances though, good intentions are not enough; our actions have to be appropriate as well! Especially being that, at times, our good intentions can be misconstrued when accompanied by the wrong action! Many a marriage has gone sour even though it started out with good intentions. Hashem knows a person's intentions, but spouses react to actions and behaviors.

So we start out with good intentions. We want to provide our spouse with whatever s/he needs, but we have no idea what that could be. Resourceful as we are, we use our hunch to decide what that may be. How disappointing and frustrating it is when our spouse makes us feel we were totally off the mark. But chances are we were indeed off mark. After all, we don't even know where that mark is! It would have been purely accidental had we actually been on target! How is it possible to provide someone with his/her needs if we have no idea what they are?

When we see that even though we're trying to help our spouse s/he only gets frustrated, let's get the hint: we're missing the point! Our getting frustrated in return will do little to enhance our relationship. It will only serve to further entrench the feelings of mutual frustration and misunderstanding.

Often, we don't know what our spouse needs. How should we? As much as we have in common, we're still different people. We must intentionally learn it! Marriage — the school of life — is like grade school: if we don't study or do our homework, we risk failing. We need to study our spouse in order to get to know his/her true needs, wants, and preferences.

So next time there's a mishap, pause and think. What was it that s/he really wanted? How did we fail to provide it? If we feel stuck and we can't figure it out, we should be brave and ask. It might be uncomfortable, but it's definitely the lesser of the two evils. And we should ask in a way that will show that we really care and truly want to know. We can then get to work. Chances are we'll be amazed at the results! There will be so much less hurt to deal with and we'll have more time to enjoy married life!

Additionally, the theory of reciprocity suggests that our spouse will try to reciprocate our caring. What more can we ask for?

We can have a happy and fulfilling relationship, but we need to get to know our partner first!

INTERPERSONAL EMPOWERMENT

ENJOY YOUR POWER
OF INFLUENCE!

Z alman was a regular, run-of-the-mill *bachur*. There was nothing spectacular or outstanding about him. That is, besides for his warm and endearing smile. Zalman made it his business to smile and to greet all the *bachurim* who crossed his path. It had become second nature to him and he didn't give it much thought.

Some ten years after he left yeshiva, Zalman bumped into Baruch, an old classmate of his. Baruch confided that back in the days when they were in yeshiva, he was going through a tough period at home. His mood and motivation were in the dumps, spending time there in the company of his self-esteem. This directly influenced his yeshiva life. His disinterest in learning cost him his *chavrusos* and his depressed mood cost him his friends. He was surrounded by darkness from all sides. The only light that illuminated the dense darkness was Zalman's smile and friendly greeting. This ray of light helped Baruch prevent the glimmer of hope from being extinguished.

Upon seeing the immense power of a simple greeting and smile, Baruch took it upon himself to do likewise. With time, others have followed.

TORAH LESSON

When discussing the laws of the liability for fire, the Torah describes in detail how a fire could get out of control and move on to destroy one thing after the other.[52] The Ohr HaChaim says that this description could be hinting to the destruction and devastation caused by the sins of the wicked.

When people sin, they don't only harm themselves, they cause damage to the whole world.

The first to suffer are the young children who die for the sins of the adults.

When that's not enough of atonement, the tzaddikim die as a korban for the generation.

When even that is not enough, the wrath of Hashem spills onto the whole generation.

In the end, however, the wicked will be held accountable for every single death and for every bit of suffering they caused with their transgressions.

We are all connected and we need to remember that!

LIFE LESSON

Who cares about what we do?

Everyone! Believe it or not, our sphere of influence is immense. We might not sport a bald head and long earlobes, we might not personify a Buddha, and we might not be worshipped by multitudes of people. Yet, every one of our moves possesses power, much more than all the fake

---

52   *Shemos* 22:5.

gods out there. Our every action could impact millions of people! Now, that's enormous power!

We thought we were regular people. How did we get hold of so much power? How did we get ourselves into such a big mess?

Well, we didn't. We were placed into it! And there is precious little we can do to extricate ourselves from it. Hashem created humans in such a way that we're constantly receiving and internalizing messages from everything that's happening around us. At the same time, we're also heavily involved in broadcasting messages, which are then picked up by the sensitive receptors of others. So even without our being aware of it, there is a nonstop data exchange taking place right under our noses!

Every single word we utter and every one of our behaviors sends a message that is picked up by others. It could influence them either positively or negatively. Their behaviors then influence others. So by this amazing ripple effect, our area of influence extends way beyond the people we actually meet. We're entangled in this worldwide web with no means to free ourselves from it.

True, we had no say in the decision to be plunged into this high data traffic intersection, but who says we have to free ourselves from it?

Who wants to live in such a busy area, you ask?

Well, let's just think about it. We're at the nerve center of a worldwide communications network. We possess power! Many media outlets and promotional enterprises would dole out fortunes for this real estate hotspot. Let's not naïvely undermine its value! Rather, let's cash in on it!

So now that we've decided to stay put, let's make the most of our exposure. Let's remember that we are constantly broadcasting, we are continuously on air and all of our communications, verbal and non-verbal, are being picked up.

With this newfound conscious awareness, we can make intelligent decisions about what our broadcasts should consist of.

We can decide to broadcast positivity and spread good feelings. We could do it by doling out generous helpings of positive comments and remarks. We could communicate encouragement and support with a genuine smile and a show of understanding and caring. We have the ability to create an atmosphere of conviviality and camaraderie almost singlehandedly! We only need to start it and be consistent about it; others will pick it up and pass it on.

Now, it may call for some investment of thought, willpower, and perseverance, but that's the way it is with any position of power. It's easy to corrupt power, and it takes a concerted effort to use it positively. But it pays! What goes around comes around. When we are instrumental in making the people around us more positive, we ourselves will benefit. Our receptors will pick up their positivity and that will in turn influence our positivity. So we're really doing it for ourselves! The best part of it all? It's free!

Light is powerful; create even a little bit of light and it'll enlighten many people!

ORDER IN THE COURT!

Shmuel was at a loss. He somehow always found himself caught in the crossfire. Going to his parents for Shabbos should have been a pleasurable experience, yet it always ended up being anything but.

It would start already on Thursday with his wife whining about how his mother had only negative things to say about her. She felt her every move was scrutinized and judged. Shabbos itself was almost unbearable. The air was rife with misunderstanding and hurt emotions, on both sides. On the way home, his wife would usually cry at how her *shvigger* mistreated her and constantly criticized her for everything.

Shmuel's mother, on the other hand, would complain to Shmuel of how hard she tried to build a relationship with his wife who was just so aloof. She considered herself better than the rest of the family and resisted joining their ranks. She was always in her room because she considered herself superior and felt it was beneath her dignity to mingle with the family.

Shmuel knew that both his mother and his wife were perhaps being a tad judgmental and they were not giving each other a chance. However, after five years of marriage, he'd given up on ever seeing any change.

TORAH LESSON

The Torah commands judges to render a *mishpat tzedek*, a true verdict.[53] The Ohr HaChaim explains how a judge could reach a true decision. When the judge ponders the case, he should remove from before his eyes the actual litigants. He shouldn't think in terms of the arguments they present. Instead, the judge should thoroughly dissect and examine the issue purely for the sake of knowing the law. Once he clarifies the halachah, he can go back and rule truthfully.

The Ohr HaChaim continues and says this is the best way to ensure that the ruling is just. Otherwise, when the judge deliberates the law with his thoughts on the two litigants, it's very difficult not to gravitate even somewhat to one side more than the other. Once that happens, it's much less likely that the ruling would be one of justice and fairness, especially when the case is not so clear-cut and calls for the judge's power of logic.

Thus, we see how once personal feelings get involved, the person's sense of right and wrong can be blurred.

LIFE LESSON

How would you feel sitting in the judge's seat?

Let's allow our imaginations to wander for a moment. You're in a courtroom surrounded by many people. The court attendant bangs on

53   *Devarim* 16:18.

the table and announces, "All rise! His honor, Judge XYZ presiding." It takes you but a moment to realize that he has mentioned your name. You're the judge! You have been called upon to preside over this court-room. You will be meting out sentences and deciding the fates of those brought before you. Whether they'll be declared innocent or guilty will be your decision. What a responsibility!

In truth, there is no need to tap into our fertile imagination for we really are judges. We are constantly passing judgments! All day every day we scrutinize and judge the people we encounter and the actions we observe. We might not be wearing the traditional black robe, and we're not presiding over an oak-paneled courtroom, but we're judges none-theless. In fact, few professional judges get to weigh in on as many cases as we do on a daily basis. With such an impressive judicial background, we ought to be nominated for a seat in the Supreme Court!

Many of our judgments are inconsequential — they're merely a reflection of our mindset. However, at times we can quite literally ruin lives with our hasty judgments. Sometimes, we don't think enough be-fore condemning people, not even offering them a fair trial and a chance to defend themselves! How many marriages have been damaged, how many promising *shidduchim* derailed, and how many great friendships were broken up due to other people's unfair judgments. Not only are our judgments powerful, they have the potential to be fatal!

Besides for not offering a fair trial, we might even be guilty of pass-ing unfair verdicts. Often we hear two identical stories and yet we view them very differently based on our perceptions of the people involved. For example, don't mothers and mothers-in-law have two very different sets of laws?

Being fair people, how are our judgments so twisted sometimes? It might just be because we seldom evaluate the act itself. Rather, we judge the people involved! So then of course we judge them differently. It all depends on our relationship with each of them!

Why do we work so hard? It surely takes a lot of energy and commit-ment to be on call for judge duty 24/7. As soon as we observe anyone doing anything we don't like, we need to drop everything, convene the court, and quickly pass judgment. What a responsibility! Why don't we leave the hard work to others while we sit back and enjoy a comfortable relationship with those around us?

Even when we feel truly irked by a specific action, we need not feel pressured to judge the person. We can just evaluate the action. Let's maintain our positive outlook on people and try to focus only on the actual thing that's bothering us. Let's imagine the bothersome scenario played out by people we don't know. Would it still bother us so much? This can help us determine whether it is the act or the person that truly bothers us. Usually, by depersonalizing the act, the irksome feelings will diminish considerably.

At times, we might wonder how we can refrain from judging people. How can we not form negative opinions of them when they're behaving that way? We're not even judging them; we're simply labeling their behavior! They are the ones causing themselves the damage!

At those times, we'd do well to remember that people do the best they can. Given their set of circumstances, their perception, their background, and their way of thinking, they're doing their best. Don't pass judgment. Rather, pass up judging!

Judging others might help us feel superior while understanding others will truly make us better!

COMPETITION IS NOT GOOD FOR BUSINESS!

I n the shadows of the towering Mt. Olympus, masses of people were celebrating jubilantly. The games had been amazing and the competition had been fierce. All contestants had pushed themselves past their limits in order to win the honorary wreath of olive leaves. These were no simple games; it was Greece's most celebrated event. Even warring city-states laid down their arms and came together as one people for this affair. The event drew a whopping forty thousand people! The Olympic Games was not something to be missed! The outcome of those games would help shape Greece's social scene until the next Olympic Games. The towns where the winners resided would receive elevated social status and it would even boost the image for the entire city-state. Surely a reason to celebrate!

This year's games would surely be remembered for a long time due to the odd turn of events. The pankration game had been especially ferocious as the two opponents fought like their very lives depended on winning, which they really did. In the end, Arrhichion of Phigalia won the competition but lost his life in the process. His opponent had locked him in a chokehold and Arrhichion, desperate to loosen it, broke his opponent's toe. The opponent nearly passed out from pain and submitted, but when the referee raised Arrhichion's hand, he realized that the latter was dead. His body was nonetheless crowned with the olive wreath and taken back to Phigalia where it was given a hero's welcome.

Arrhichion had, indeed, given his all to win — even his life.

TORAH LESSON

Rivka was afraid and confused by the strangeness of her pregnancy. Shem informed her (in the name of Hashem) that she was carrying twins who would go on to form separate nations: "And one nation from the other will strengthen itself."[54] The Ohr HaChaim points out that two nations can, theoretically, live side by side peacefully. Thus, the fact that Yaakov and Eisav would form separate nations shouldn't necessarily preclude living in harmony with each other. That was not reason enough for their prenatal bickering.

However, Hashem added, there would never be equality between those two nations. There would be continuous struggle between them, each one trying to overpower the other. They will compete for superiority and they will each want to see the other's downfall. This, in effect, would snuff out any and every feeling of companionship and brotherly love. It's impossible to love someone while trying at the same time to rise above him and bring about his downfall. It just doesn't work.

---

54   *Bereishis* 25:23.

LIFE LESSON

Competition is good for business, right?

Well, it might be. For most businesses, at least. However, it's surely not the case with the "human resources" business. It wreaks havoc with our egos, rocks our self-esteem, robs our confidence, induces anxiety, and inhibits positive social interaction.

In fact, competition is a disservice to everyone involved, winner and loser. Due to the competitive society that we live in, we've become hung up on such trivialities as first, fastest, or best.

Does it really matter if we're at the top?

Does it say anything of us, or does it just indicate that others are less than us?

Let's say we weren't first or best; does that really mean our accomplishments are worth less? It's quite possible that we have extended ourselves to our limits, that we had accomplished great things so why should we be unfair to ourselves?

Additionally, when we use competition as our barometer for measuring our self-worth, we risk hurting our true inner value system. It's mind-boggling to think how low we could be tempted to stoop when we're driven by competition. How many times do we go against our morals and how often do we redefine our ethics and skew our judgment just because of this competition thing? In a moment of sobriety, we would be utterly ashamed of the way we behaved during the competition-induced stupor.

David was a nice and friendly *bachur*. He decided to start waking up at 5 a.m. in order to put in some extra time learning. Shmuel, his roommate, asked him to wake him as well, as he too wanted to have an early morning *seder*. David felt very threatened by the possibility of competition. Not only did he not wake up Shmuel, he actively derided Shmuel to others. David's early morning *seder* is long history, but his regret over his treatment of Shmuel hasn't passed yet.

Surveys have shown that performance competition in the workplace increases unethical behaviors such as sabotage, mistreatment, and intimidation. In other settings as well, it has been shown that the drive to be on top provides a fertile breeding ground for selfishness, jealousy, truth distortion, cheating, and aggressiveness.

When we get stuck on being best, first, and top, not only are we betraying our true inner selves, we also start devaluing ourselves and others. We stop valuing people for who they are; we only value their accomplishments, and even then only if they were on top or the best. In fact, we start worshipping accomplishment and despising non-accomplished people, even ourselves!

This, understandably, creates within us a tremendous amount of anxiety as we try to push ourselves past our limits just to prevent the self-loathing. When it doesn't work (because there will, inevitably, be people more successful than we are), we become frustrated with ourselves and we just don't feel like trying again.

Let's think about it: are we only worth something if we're more than others? Does that mean that we'll forever be worthless just because there will always be someone better than we are?

Now, let's have a look at the interpersonal side of our competition. We've learned to lull our consciousness into complacency by fooling ourselves into believing that we could be good friends even while we're competing. But that's humanly impossible! We can't be someone's friend and wish him all the best when we're desperately hoping that he won't do so well and we'll be able to overtake him. It just doesn't make sense! We would need to have multiple personality disorder to accomplish that!

But what about the driving force that competition affords us? Doesn't it help us to try harder and accomplish great things? Why should we compromise on a method that has proven itself to be effective?

We need not compromise on anything! True, when we see other's success, it arouses in us the drive to succeed as well. Chazal said, "The jealousy of scholars increases wisdom."[55]

The point is that we could use others' success as a source of inspiration and as an example for us to follow. We can learn effective techniques and methods by studying others. We can use all that

---

55   *Bava Basra* 21a.

as motivation for ourselves to work better and harder. It need not be about *what* the others have accomplished, but *how* they accomplished it!

Let's draw inspiration from others, but compete
only against ourselves!

CONFIDENT ABOUT CONFIDENTIALITY

There's an oval room in Washington D.C. where many important meetings take place. It's generally assumed that the things discussed there are confidential. Perhaps it's the room's unique shape that's supposed to prevent the escape of secrets.

However, all this was nixed when President Nixon decided to install a secret recording system in the room. Without anyone knowing it, everything uttered in the Oval Office was now being recorded. Nixon had no compunctions about breaching confidentiality for the sake of his personal ambitions. (There were other presidents who also had recording systems installed, but Nixon's was the first system that recorded everything automatically). As the saying goes, "What goes around comes around," because in the end, Nixon himself was the one who suffered the most from this breach of confidentiality.

When the Watergate scandal was discovered, the federal investigators had little evidence to link it to the president. At first, it seemed Nixon would be able to steer clear of the whole mess and only lower ranking officials would shoulder the whole burden. Then, however, it came to light that there were recordings from the Oval Office and the court subpoenaed them. Nixon's own confidentiality was breached. The gates opened wide and all the ugly water came pouring out. The handwriting was right there on the wall — well, the reel — pointing to the president's direct involvement.

TORAH LESSON

In many places in the Torah we find the adjoining phrases, "And Hashem spoke to Moshe to convey. Speak to the Bnei Yisrael." The Ohr HaChaim asks why the Torah repeats itself by telling Moshe to convey what he was told and then commanding him to speak to Bnei Yisrael.[56] Wouldn't just one of them suffice?

The Ohr HaChaim answers it with a Gemara. The Gemara says that a person is prohibited from repeating anything told to him except for when he receives explicit authorization by the person who told it to him that he may share the information.[57] Otherwise, it is deemed confidential. Thus, Hashem first had to give Moshe permission to repeat what was told to him. Then He actually commanded him to say it.

LIFE LESSON

We know how to keep a secret, right?

Um, let's think again. How many times do we share bits of information that others have entrusted us with, sometimes without even

---

56   *Shemos* 25:2.
57   *Yuma* 4b.

realizing? Our sensitivity not to divulge anything told to us has become somewhat compromised. It would seem we're adapting to the spirit of our time, best expressed by the motto of mass media, "The public has the right to know."

In fact, by the urgency with which some people publicize others' personal details, it would appear we're actually on an all-out crusade for social liberty. We want to ensure that the public's rights are upheld. Not only does the public have the right to know, some people try to see to it that they will actually get to know everything.

It is well known that the best way to obtain information about anyone in our communities is though "the grapevine." It's laden with information, most of it never intended for the public. It's actually amazing that the grapevine doesn't buckle under the immense weight of its load! Whenever we're not careful enough and we allow some information to leak, we're watering the grapevine.

Of course, we never intentionally divulge anything that was shared with us in confidence. We try to keep secret the things we've been warned not to tell anyone. We've just lost our appreciation of the importance of keeping private even those bits of information that weren't accompanied by explicit warnings. Additionally, the ease with which we sometimes talk about others could cause us to inadvertently slip up from time to time and leak even those very private things.

In the spirit of secular culture, you need not overly agitate yourself about this; you can just write it off as an accident. We believe we need to keep our eyes focused on the big picture. In the greater scheme of things, it's surely no more than a minor slip-up for the sake of ensuring that the public's right to know is respected.

At times we might be plagued by our conscience and feel guilty for wronging other people by unwittingly spilling their secrets, but we need not worry. We can take solace in the thought that in all probability they too reveal our secrets. So not only are we watering the grapevine with other's secrets, our own secrets are also traveling along that very vine. How encouraging! What a great way to personally contribute to the social liberty cause!

It's possible that some of us won't feel placated with the reassurance that many aspects of our lives are aired publicly. This would mean that we're not fully convinced of the merits of the cause. In that case, we might just be better off refraining from discussing other people's personal lives completely, whether they requested we keep it a secret or not. Besides, we know full well that it's the right thing to do in any case!

What are we afraid of? Well, if we decide to face up to the challenge and stop sharing everything others tell us, there are some problems that are sure to come up.

Firstly, we'll be blatantly violating the public's right to know.

Secondly, and more importantly, we might be stuck with no topics for conversation and no fodder to feed the gossip machines. Life will surely become bland and boring.

While the former is chiefly a concern for the liberally conscious, the latter is a serious worry for the avid social conversationalists among us. Truth be told, there is no simple solution to this issue.

While it's true that we might go through an adjustment period until we devise new forms of socializing, it will be well worth the wait! Our social interactions will take on a more positive tone. We might also find ourselves engaging in more stimulating conversations about real things instead of gossip and innuendo. Chances are that we'll also feel much better about ourselves knowing that we possess the inner strength to withstand the temptation. As for the cause of social liberty and the public's right to know, we can worry about that when we're done with our personal work.

Let's have confidence in our ability to be confidential, and others will also have confidence in us!

HOW CAN WE OVERCOME HATRED?

veryone on the block knew about it.

The people in shul knew about it.

In fact, who didn't know about it?

There was longstanding animosity between the Weiss and Schwartz families. There was no active fighting, just an invisible chasm separating the two families. No one was sure how it had started, but it was an established reality. The *rav* had tried on more than one occasion to get involved; he even once succeeded in getting the two men to sit down at one table, but that was as far as he got. Others who had tried were also quick to learn that it was a waste of time and effort.

Things came to a head when the Schwartz daughter was rejected from the high school of her choice. They later learned that it was Mrs. Weiss's doing. She had informed the principal that she would pull her daughters out if the Schwartz girl was accepted. This was too much, and Mrs. Schwartz decided to put an end to the fighting. She tried talking to her husband about tearing down the walls of animosity, but she just encountered a wall of pain. Mr. Schwartz forcefully declared that there was no way he would reconcile with Mr. Weiss after the latter had hurt him so strongly. No amount of reasoning or pleading was able to move Mr. Schwartz from his position. From his point of view the topic was closed, never to be reopened.

TORAH LESSON

Why is Hashem opposed to peculiar forms of idolatry such as relieving oneself in honor of Pe'or or stoning the Markulis? Aren't they degrading for the idol? Additionally, the Ohr HaChaim points out, this prohibition could lead someone to make two very wrong inferences:[58]

- One might think that these strange rituals are in actuality a worthy form of worship, and thus Hashem resents them being done to idols.
- One could think that while these forms of worship are surely despicable, Hashem is only upset because the people are not serving Him in ways appropriate for serving Hashem.

Both misinterpretations can be very misleading.

If one believes that Hashem actually desires those odd forms of worship, he might, Heaven forbid, want to serve Hashem in a similar manner.

As for the second mistake, that could lead one to believe that so long as he is fulfilling his duties to Hashem, he can also relieve himself at the Pe'or rest area.

The Torah, therefore, says that neither of the two reasons is true. Hashem simply despises everything that the nations do for their gods, whether the action is despicable or respectable.

---

58   *Devarim* 12:29-31.

LIFE LESSON

If we feel hatred towards someone, there is obviously a reason for it. What then does *sinas chinam*, baseless hatred, mean? Isn't it an oxymoron?

There must surely be something about the other person that causes us to feel we just can't stand them! Sometimes, just thinking of that person causes our blood to boil or go cold, and we feel discomfort all over the place. At other times, we simply feel a distinct sense of dislike toward another. It surely can't be baseless!

The truth is hatred, in any form, has very good reason! Hatred does us an amazing service. It serves as a cover-up to bury our vulnerability. It protects us from having to face some of our weak points.

Let's explore the amazing benefits of hate. The first stop on our itinerary will be at the Pit of Envy. As soon as we enter this pit, we tend to feel lower and inferior to the person we envy. Our egos often have a bad reaction to this sudden change of climate. This sense of inferiority — that someone has more than we do or is more than we are — is very unhealthy for our egos.

Our immune system automatically kicks in and helps us develop antibodies towards that person. We start feeling a sense of loathing toward him/her. The feelings of dislike trigger our minds to start finding faults in the person to justify those feelings. Our minds are creative enough to churn out many reasons: he is so materialistic, he is so shallow, he has such poor *middos*, etc.

In reality, another's shortcomings have no reason to bother us. Rather, our feeling of hatred toward him affords us a sense of superiority over that person and it lifts us out of the pit. Our egos are safe once again.

For the second part of our trip we'll hop over to the overlook above the municipal dumping ground. At times, our hatred is laced with revulsion; we might feel a certain sense of disgust as we look down on the other. Now, this too is a cover-up. We might be afraid to associate with someone we perceive as inferior, lest we too be perceived as inferior by association. When we project a feeling of dislike toward someone we are sort of lifting ourselves up higher so that no connection is ever made. Thus, we are safe from the danger of being underestimated.

Now that we've successfully completed our trip, we can decide to go back home and just keep doing what we've been doing all along. Why should we care that we're surrounded by massive fields of negative energy produced by our hatred? True, it hurts us in so many ways, but we're paralyzed by the fear of uncovering our feelings of inferiority! We're not ready to dig through the mounds of hatred just to uncover its source — the very things we've worked so hard to bury! We'd prefer to leave everything the way it is.

However, the brave and adventurous among us can continue the trip by hiking the self-discovery trail. We start out with the recognition that there is in fact a source to our hatred. In some way, this person is making us feel inferior. Once we've passed this major hurdle, we're ready to explore how and why we actually perceive this person as a threat to our egos. By this time, most of our hatred will have disappeared without any active effort (perhaps out of sheer exhaustion?).

We are now ready for the final leg of our trip. All we need to do now is realize that there's no real connection between us and the other person. They are neither higher nor lower than us; they are just different. Whether we look up at them or down at them is not based on reality — it's all in our minds. We can decide to look straight at them and enjoy a peaceful life. After all, the hatred was really not about them, but about us!

One funny trick to overcoming hatred is to inwardly start wishing the best for the very person we hate. This will cause our brains to process that s/he is not a threat to us. The animosity will disappear without our even noticing it.

Hatred is like a shield; it's protective but cumbersome. When we feel secure with ourselves, we don't need the shield.

MAKE YOUR ADVICE
VALUABLE

r. Teller was the perfect chairman; he loved to man the whole world from his chair. Mr. Teller had sound advice to offer about everything. He just knew how to do things better than everyone else. He believed it would be beneficial if he were to take charge of various *mosdos* and organizations in order to correct all the problems in the current systems. Mr. Teller also had invaluable advice to offer for all elected politicians; he operated a free advice *gemach* for the numerous community *askanim*. Mr. Teller would always say wistfully, "If only people would listen to me, the world would be a much better place."

Convincing as Mr. Teller sounded, years flew by and he still had little to show for his effort. He did manage to earn the contempt of many activists due to his steady flow of unsolicited advice, which they construed as criticism. With time, Mr. Teller became frustrated at the lack of positive results for all the effort he was investing in forming and expressing his expert advice. Truth be told, people did find it entertaining to listen to Mr. Teller, but not to accept and follow his advice.

TORAH LESSON

Yisro felt there was need for improvement in Moshe's judiciary system. He believed that Moshe could not handle the whole burden himself. There was a need for a complex judiciary hierarchy in order to handle the numerous litigations of such a large nation. Yisro was a professional advisor and political strategist, and he knew how to successfully plan and implement such a hierarchy. However, before he started lecturing his son-in-law on how to do things better, he inquired of Moshe why he ran things the way he did.

The Ohr HaChaim explains in detail the dialogue that took place between Yisro and his venerated son-in-law.[59] Before making any recommendations, Yisro tried to truly understand Moshe's reasoning for his mode of operation. He made sure to analyze every nuance of Moshe's reasoning. Only once he had discussed it with Moshe and was confident that he understood the advantages as well as the shortcomings of the current system did Yisro unfold his plan. His plan was designed in such a way that it sufficiently addressed the inadequacies in the current system while at the same time incorporating in it all the benefits of the existing arrangement.

LIFE LESSON

Why have words become cheap?

Because of inflation, of course! Let's think about it. How often do we magnanimously offer someone a penny for his thoughts? However,

---

59   *Shemos* 18:15-18.

should he actually dare take us up on our offer and put in his two cents, something strange will usually happen: we'll totally disregard his opinion and consider it worthless. A minute earlier we were ready to pay for it, but now we don't even want it for free. Now that's called serious inflation!

It's kind of puzzling when we think about what's been happening in the advice industry. In recent years, advice has become such a precious commodity that people are ready to shell out fortunes just to obtain some of it. Governments squander taxpayers' money to attain it. Shrewd business tycoons invest in it. Even simple, run-of-the-mill folks use their hard-earned money to get hold of some of it. Think tanks work hard to produce some more of it. In fact, advice has become a multi-billion dollar industry.

While we are paying through our teeth for some crumbs of advice, it would stand to reason that we would try to grab as much free advice as we could lay our hands on. But here is where our fickleness comes to a head: not only do we not try to snatch up every droplet of free advice that comes our way, we actually detest it! We humans surely are strange creatures!

Why indeed do we demonstrate such abhorrence to free advice? Isn't there a possibility that we would gain some insight from it even if it was unsolicited?

The answer might very well be that we seldom receive free advice. Of course people bombard us all the time with their opinions, but that's not advice. None of these unsolicited advisors even thought of investing any time or effort into truly and thoroughly understanding our issues. They weren't privy to our many deliberations and predicaments. And if they don't know the true nature of the problem, they can't possibly offer counsel! That's not advice, it's gibberish! The only thing people accomplish when they put in their two cents is that they may cause us to feel like two cents. We might actually feel hurt by what we perceive as a lack of sensitivity to our dilemma. Is there any wonder that we detest it?

Yes, there are times when we see a friend or loved one struggling in a certain area and we feel we have some valuable advice for them. We feel it could be a real game changer if they would hear what we have to say.

Do we have to withhold our advice just because they didn't ask us for it?

The answer is an unequivocal no!

We need only ascertain that we really are in possession of the right advice. For that, we need to make an effort to find out the true issue at hand. Without being too pushy we could let our friend know that it's possible we have some information they might find valuable. When they're ready to hear, we can gently inquire about the pertinent details. We'll then be in a much better position to judge whether our recommendations could be of any use. Once we do offer our counsel, it's time for us to back off. Being pushy and pestering the person to follow our advice has nothing to do with helping out!

Advice is very valuable. It should be dispensed sparingly and only when it's really needed!

HOLY WAR?!

Mrs. P. was very concerned. Fifteen-year-old Shmuel was about to head off to sleepaway camp. Shmuel wasn't just any son; he was her pride. Unlike his brothers, Shmuel, it seemed, wasn't negatively impacted by the family's wealth and social standing. He was a serious boy, truly into his learning and *avodas Hashem*.

Yitzi, from the simple family across the street, would be attending the same camp. Yitzi had been involved in some mischief with Shmuel's older brother Duvi, and Mrs. P. was sure that her precious Duvi wasn't to blame for the mischief. The only possible explanation was that Yitzi was a negative influence on her children. Therefore, Mrs. P. warned her Shmuel not to sleep in the same room as Yitzi.

In his extreme piety and *avodas Hashem*, Shmuel made sure to let everyone know that his mother forbade him to sleep in the same room as Yitzi. Other aspiring *ovdei Hashem* quickly joined in. It didn't take long for Yitzi to become the outcast in camp, shunned by everyone — all in the name of *avodas Hashem*.

The wounds that Yitzi's soul and ego sustained that summer were nearly fatal. One arrogant mother's misplaced contempt nearly ruined an innocent boy's life. It was only through Hashem's great mercy that Yitzi didn't drop out. The wounds remained open and they festered for many years.

Even many years later, Shmuel was still enveloped in his piety and wouldn't even greet Yitzi. Perhaps he was still afraid of being negatively influenced through even a minor interaction.

TORAH LESSON

The Torah relates how Bnei Yisrael caught a blasphemer and brought him to Moshe to find out how to punish him. "And Moshe spoke to Bnei Yisrael and they hauled the blasphemer outside of the encampment and they stoned him, and Bnei Yisrael did as Hashem had commanded Moshe."[60]

The Ohr HaChaim asks, Why is it important for the Torah to state that Bnei Yisrael did as Hashem had commanded Moshe? By relating that they stoned the blasphemer, don't we already see that they did as they were commanded?

The Ohr HaChaim explains that the Torah is relaying something very profound. Chazal tell us that the blasphemer was of dubious lineage and he was embroiled in a fight with a kosher "purebred" member of the Klal Yisrael. One could therefore think that Bnei Yisrael had an axe to grind with this illegitimate member and their motives for bringing him to justice weren't all that pure. Surely they only had Hashem in mind, but maybe they did it with just a pinch of misplaced zealotry. Hence, the Torah found it necessary to tell us that Bnei Yisrael did as Hashem had commanded Moshe. Their intentions were completely pure; untainted

---

60   *Vayikra* 24:23.

by even a minute sense of revenge.

LIFE LESSON

What is worth fighting for?

It's hard to say. Our little world offers a plethora of worthy and holy causes we can fight for. And holy wars are not strictly the domain of bloodthirsty terrorists. In fact, many of us are actively involved in some holy war or another. Be it the chutzpah of the neighbor's children, the guy who lets his cell phone ring in shul, the wardrobe of the family down the block, the other *chassidus*, the *chinuch* system, etc.

Interestingly enough, it's not always clear-cut who the holy one is. In many holy wars, each side claims to be the holy one, battling the other purely for the sake of Hashem. The holiness of these wars is sometimes even used to justify numerous transgressions that are done in the process. People write the mitzvos off as war casualties. It's really amazing how we can defy Hashem's commands for His sake!

Of course, many of us might not appreciate the loftiness of physically and emotionally hurting others for the sake of some supposed ultimate truth. Thus, we really would do best to steer clear from the battlefield. Let's leave the fighting to the skilled warriors.

The time we gain by dodging the so-called holy draft could be put to good use. We could use that time to learn how to appreciate differences of opinion and taste. They are, after all, part and parcel of the human social experience. Those differences often lead to the formation of a variety of sub-groups with each group developing its own character and way of doing things. Differences do not necessarily mean invalidation. Think about it: wouldn't the world be a very boring place if everyone thought and dressed the same way? We ought to appreciate the people who are different from us for adding spice to our life!

There are times when we are called upon by our leaders to take a stance in opposition to a given group. We ought to practice extreme caution during those times lest it deteriorate into a holy war with numerous casualties. Let's remember that zealotry in all of its various forms, whether individual or community-wide, is a very tricky and sticky issue.

It could easily spiral out of control and become a jihad where spilling other people's blood is justified in the name of "The Cause."

In truth, zealotry ought to be viewed as an elevated form of *avodas Hashem*. True zealotry stems from a burning desire to fulfill Hashem's commandments — all of them, even the ones that are *bein adam l'chaveiro*, between man and fellow man. Zealotry is all about pain, not about anger. It's about reacting to a deep inner pain that we feel when Hashem's honor is trampled. Zealotry is about the act and not about the person! If it's a deep anger that we feel towards the other, then we know that it's not about zealotry!

When in doubt, just take the easy way out. Let's not expose ourselves to the perils of a so-called holy war.

Let's do for Hashem's sake in ways that will make Hashem happy!

SOMETHING TO SMILE ABOUT

The situation in the D. household left much to be desired. There were lots of bad feelings between husband and wife. Neither of them could point to anything specific or tangible that bothered them about their spouse. There was just a toxic air in the house that seemed to poison their every interaction.

Actually, they kept their interactions to a minimum. They each went their own way trying as much as possible not to get in the other's way. On numerous occasions they had decided to work on their marriage, but they couldn't pinpoint any specific issues to work on so things just continued the way they were. The situation kept on deteriorating and it looked like they were quickly approaching the point of no return.

Then, husband and wife decided to try and focus on their communication, not even so much on the verbal part of communication as on the nonverbal one. They started smiling at each other and looking agreeably at the actions of the other. At first, the change was hardly noticeable, but ever so slowly, the toxic air disappeared. In its place came acceptance and appreciation.

TORAH LESSON

In describing the necessary code of conduct for judges, the Torah reveals to us some of the intricacies and complexities of interpersonal interactions.[61] The Ohr HaChaim points out how the Torah demands of a *dayan* to exercise extreme sensitivity with regards to his nonverbal communication.

The judge should not show a friendly face and make eye contact with one party while diverting his eyes from the other party. He should be sure to make equal eye contact. In fact, the Ohr HaChaim says, it's best for the judge to refrain from making any eye contact whatsoever. There is always the risk of one litigant imagining that the judge looked somewhat more favorably at his opponent. He would then lose his motivation to even present his arguments, as he'd be sure that the case had been decided in the favor of his opponent.

LIFE LESSON

We are sensitive, aren't we?

We might be too sensitive to admit it since after all, sensitivity in adulthood is generally shunned. We like to think of ourselves as being made of stronger stuff, but that might not necessarily reflect reality. We tend to be heavily invested in jealously guarding our oh-so-fragile egos. We measure and deduce, infer and interpret movements, comments, and facial expressions of those we come in contact with to be sure that

---

61   *Devarim* 1:15.

our egos haven't been attacked. Not that we're sensitive, we simply need to know what others think of us. Self understood.

While we're actively analyzing how others treated us, they might be busy doing the same thing — examining how we treated them. It would seem that we're all involved in this cross examination. No need to be sensitive and feel offended by this. Everyone likes to be treated with respect and recognition; it's part of the human experience.

So with the recognition that we all share this common interest, wouldn't it make life so much simpler to make some sort of treaty? We should collectively decide to do our best not to hurt others. After all, we really do know how much it hurts when our egos are bruised. Additionally, we tend to reflect back the mood and attitude that others feel towards us. Hence, when we're nice and respectful toward others, we stand a much better chance of them returning the gesture. A real win-win! So, let's go for it!

Of course, being nice includes speaking nicely, but it's much more than that. If we were to view each of us as an individual country, then our mouth would be our State Department. When we speak, we could formulate our words in ways that are politically correct. We have the ability to control what we say and what to leave unsaid. Our words don't necessarily reflect our true inner feelings or beliefs. Our eyes and facial expressions, on the other hand, are our media outlet. They uncover and air our true inner beliefs for all to see. They tell the story of our true feelings and emotions. We could keep our mouths closed and yet speak volumes through our eyes and facial expressions!

In fact, we communicate considerably more nonverbally than we do verbally! Furthermore, nonverbal communication is very powerful, possibly even more powerful than spoken communication! Our facial expressions have the power to set or change the mood in a room. When we enter with a happy countenance, those around us will automatically feel in a more positive mood. Conversely, when our face conveys negativity, it will drag down the moods of those around us. The messages we send with our eyes are even more potent. They have the power to give life or to snuff out every bit of life!

In our quest to steer clear of hurting others and in our pursuit to spread positivity, let's focus on our eyes and facial expressions. Let's try to invest some effort into truly feeling more positive about others by focusing on the good in them. Our eyes will then convey our positivity and we'll be able to offer real smiles.

Let's practice making eye contact when we interact with others and looking at them with love and acceptance. Let's learn to frown at frowning and to happily wear a happy countenance! We'll make others feel good and we'll feel better ourselves too. It works like a charm. When we lift the mood of others, our mood gets lifted too. There is no better way for our egos to get a boost than to lift up someone else's ego. It really works!

If we think about it, we'd realize that we see precious little of our own face — it's mainly others who see it. We owe it to those who see our face most to leave them with a good feeling.

Our faces are public property; we have absolutely no right to deface them!

WE'RE SEEING WHATEVER WE WANT TO SEE

The yeshiva was abuzz with the news of last night's kitchen break-in. Danny was livid. He knew that the *mashgiach* was blaming him for it. Why didn't anyone trust him? Back home, he'd always been accused of everything that went wrong; he was always guilty even after being proven innocent. And now, this attitude had followed him to his new yeshiva. Was it really impossible to dispose his mark of Cain?

Danny had especially opted to attend an out-of-town yeshiva in order to be far away from the problem called home and to get a fresh start. Alas, his bad luck just seemed to follow him wherever he went. From the first day, Danny saw right through the *mashgiach*'s smile; he *knew* that the friendliness was just an act. Danny smelled foul play even when the boys tried to befriend him. He knew he couldn't be cautious enough. It was surely just a matter of time before they would start riding on his good heart and abusing his weaknesses — just like at home.

This morning, when the *mashgiach* brushed past him and greeted him with a friendly "Good morning," Danny knew right away that the *mashgiach* accused him of the break-in. The extra friendliness was definitely a setup in order to fool Danny into confessing for the crime he didn't do.

It took time and a lot of unconditional acceptance for Danny to start seeing things differently. Danny learned that it wasn't bad luck that followed him everywhere. It was really his tainted pair of eyeglasses that he made sure to bring along wherever he went. He realized that he had been reacting to his perceptions and not necessarily to reality.

TORAH LESSON

Yosef was well aware of his brothers' dislike for him. They were very honest with their feelings and they didn't cover up their negativity towards him. Why then, did Yosef stoke the flames of hatred by sharing his first dream with them? Wasn't he perceptive enough to realize that the dream's prediction of lordship would only serve to intensify their negativity towards him?

The Ohr HaChaim[62] explains it with a Gemara in *Berachos*.[63] The Gemara says that the realization of a dream is dependent upon its interpretation. Therefore, the Gemara advises, one should ask his friends to decipher the dream for him since they care about him and will give the dream a good spin, ensuring a favorable interpretation.

---

62   *Bereishis* 37:5.
63   55b.

Hence, Yosef figured that by asking his brothers to interpret his dream, he would be showing them he viewed them as the people closest to him, and that he was confident in their reciprocal love.

His brothers, on the other hand, were filtering all of Yosef's actions through their preconceived notion that he considered himself superior to them. Therefore, they perceived this dream, and his retelling of it to them, as an additional act of asserting his superiority over them. This, in turn, only intensified their hatred.

LIFE LESSON

How do the general media always find sensational things to write about?

It's quite possible that it's all in the glasses they wear, their perception. They possess the unique ability to find whatever they want to find. They're experts at embedding their own biased interpretations into seemingly neutral statements. They're also very good at quoting others' statements out of context in order to make something sensational.

Sometimes, we seem to be in possession of those unique media skills. Let's take a minute to think about it.

Do we generally react to what's actually being said to us or to our perception of what was said? Should we allow ourselves some time to think before getting all worked up about things said to us, we might realize that the statement wasn't all that bad. At times, it might even have been intended as a compliment! It's our media tainted glasses that portray a distorted picture.

But, we could argue, why should we waste our media talents?

Actually, there really is no need for our talents to die the obscure death of an undecorated hero. We could use those very capabilities and turn them around to help us build and enhance friendships! We don't need to remain boringly impartial in our interpersonal interactions. With some minor cosmetic changes, we can use our talents to find more joy in life and to enhance our friendships.

Our ability to zoom in on the minute details of an interaction could be redirected to help us find something positive even in a seemingly negative remark. We can also continue taking statements out of context. We'll simply do it in ways that will promote feelings of goodwill.

It is within our power to decide how we want to perceive others. People are seldom two-dimensional, and the glasses we wear could determine which dimensions we notice. We'll enjoy a much nicer view of the world in general and people in particular once we decide to put on a prettier pair of glasses.

While it might not earn us any accolades in the reeking media industry, it will surely help us to develop a refreshing optimism. Those around us will usually perceive the change in our perception and they'll find it more enjoyable to spend time with us. Thus, we'll have even more opportunities to enjoy the beauty of mankind.

So, what's there to hesitate about? It's a win-win solution! We get to keep our amazing analytical talents and we'll lead a happier life filled with positivity and surrounded by friends! What could be better? Is there any need for more convincing? Let's go for it!

Life is the color that we paint it to be.

THE HILARIOUS
HOARDING HOAX

Mr. Zamler was lucky to be of the very organized, no-nonsense type. He owned so much stuff that life would have been total chaos had he not been organized. His closets were full of clothing — most of which have been out of circulation for quite a while. There in the closet stood sentry an impressive array of suits and shoes, witness to the rich and colorful history of men's fashions. They had dutifully served their time in their era, and yet there was no way Mr. Zamler could get himself to dispose of them.

The basement was a self-contained mini history museum; it sported a generous selection of historic artifacts. A large variety of pre-loved pieces of furniture competed for space against an amazing selection of every type of used appliances. There was also a tool corner and a generous suitcase collection of various sizes, shapes, functionalities, and periods. Many of them were useless, but it was likewise useless to try and convince Mr. Zamler to get rid of them. There was also an impressive map collection that was surely historic, affording a glimpse into life from before GPSes. Visiting Mr. Zamler's basement was a feast for the eye and an offense to the olfactory system.

He would never go and pick up useless items, but once something came into his possession, there was no way Mr. Zamler would part with it. There was always a possibility that those eyeglasses would someday come back into style. He was also convinced that there must be some poor *meshulach* who would gratefully accept an old suit. And those suitcases; if anything happened that would force them to flee, they'd definitely need every piece of luggage they could put their hands on. In truth, Mr. Zamler felt some unexplainable emotional connection to his stuff.

TORAH LESSON

Upon enumerating the things donated for the building of the *Mishkan*, the Torah divides the donations into four categories.[64] There was jewelry and gold vessels; gold; dyed wools and hides; and the rest, ranging from silver to copper to wood. Why did the Torah place jewelry as a separate category and not include it with the gold? Additionally, shouldn't silver (being a precious metal) have been grouped together with the gold?

The Ohr HaChaim explains that those four categories are arranged according to the decreasing degrees of hardship it took to part with them. In other words, the four categories represent the four levels of emotional connection people tend to feel toward their belongings. The greater one's connection the more difficult it is to part with.

At the top of the list are objects of personal use such as jewelry and clothing. One understandably tends to have a strong emotional

---

64   *Shemos* 35:22-25.

connection to those things; they can become part of one's identity, and it's hardest to part with them.

Next is gold, whose luster and intrinsic value entices people to collect it and hold on to it.

Following this are items that may not be so valuable but are rare and hard to come by, such as dyed wools in a desert.

The lowest level includes all the rest of one's belongings.

The Torah mapped out the hierarchy of the normal human attachment to one's belongings. The greater one's attachment to an item the more likely the person is to collect it and hold on to it. Thus, Hashem valued the donations accordingly.

LIFE LESSON

Why do we enjoy hoarding so much?

Who says we enjoy it? Well, if we have a closer look at our behaviors then we might admit that we are, indeed, hoarders.

We like to hoard "hurts" in great quantity; we make sure to pick them up wherever we go. We let ourselves get hurt easily and we hold on to these hurts much longer than we should, hoarding them.

It doesn't even matter whether the hurts were intentional or not. It would make a great comedy if we would be able to observe how we sometimes go out of our way to collect these hurts. We could spend copious amounts of time analyzing remarks, trying to find the one offending particle that would allow us to feel hurt. We then add it to our already prodigious collection.

Still, who says we're pathological hoarders? Maybe we're respectable collectors? After all, only hoarders are shunned and dragged to therapy. Collectors and collections, on the other hand, are looked upon positively by society.

What is the difference between collecting and hoarding?

Collecting is pleasurable and has been around for many millennia.

Collections will usually have uniting themes or sentimental value.

Hoarding, however, seldom has any logical relationship amongst the stuff amassed, and they are rarely of any true or sentimental value. Additionally, there is no pleasure involved in hoarding other than the pacification of the hoarding urge or avoidance of the pain caused by discarding something. While a great many of us would go out of our way to view certain collections, we would hardly ever find interest in hoarded goods.

Our collections of hurts have all the symptoms of a hoarding disorder. They possess no innate or sentimental value. No one else understands why we're collecting them and guarding them with such zeal and no one cares to hear about them. It only causes us distress and interferes with our social functioning. We tend to be emotionally attached to the hurts and we find it very difficult to let go.

Many of us have "open accounts" with countless people. We often remember the exact amount and timing of the various hurts. Some even keep a precise ledger on how to treat different people according to the hurts accrued in their accounts. It calls for a lot of brain power! Additionally, people seem not to understand why we're giving them the cold shoulder and they add insult to injury by perceiving us as sensitive. They start avoiding our company and now we have even more hurts to hoard and store.

Our hoarding of hurts causes our brains to get so cluttered that we have little place left to welcome positive and good feelings. Worse still, we have no one to blame for it!

Let's take a minute off our busy hoarding schedule and think about it. What are we gaining from our obsession with all this useless collection of memories of hurts?

Are the people who hurt us really so important that we should award their comments prime air time on our brain waves for months and years? Additionally, who says they actually wanted to insult us? And, if they did, they must be suffering from a bad case of insensitivity, and their comments most definitely don't deserve to be stored.

Hoarding "hurts" hurts. Collecting good feelings feels much better.

CHINUCH
EMPOWERMENT

THE PROMISING
POTENT POTION

The results of the studies were very discouraging; they left academicians and politicians befuddled. But there was no arguing with the numbers, as study after study produced similar results. It was proven that the scholastic performance of Japanese students was considerably higher than that of their American counterparts. It hurts to face reality, but there's no way to get around it.

It is believed among researchers that a combination of factors contribute to this phenomenon. One of those factors is the difference in the social structure. In Japanese culture, great emphasis is placed on the honor of the family. Kids are taught that it's important for them to perform well academically and to behave in order to bring honor to the

179

family. When a child misbehaves, he is chastised for bestowing shame upon the whole family. The sense of responsibility towards the reputation of the family prompts Japanese kids to exert themselves and perform well.

American culture, on the other hand, is hooked on individuality. It's all about each person forging his/her own path without being tied down by the unwanted baggage of family and tradition. Tradition is scorned and upholding family honor is viewed as outdated at best. With this mindset, people are prompted to do as they please and whatever they feel is good. Thus, if a student wants to hang out and neglect his school work, family honor will do little to hold him back.

TORAH LESSON

Chazal tell us that when Hashem selected Klal Yisrael to give them the Torah, the nations complained.[65] They wanted to know why they were passed over in favor of Klal Yisrael. Hashem told them, "Bring forth your pedigrees." No one was able to procure it or trace their lineage to any given family. Hashem is disdainful towards those who have no clear pedigree. Thus, the nations didn't stand a chance. The Ohr HaChaim takes it a bit further and says that the very fact that Klal Yisrael had a pedigree was enough to award them a noble stature.[66]

Hashem's contempt towards people of no clear lineage is seemingly tied with His repugnance of illegitimate marital unions. We can possibly add another reason for the importance of being aware and feeling connected to one's lineage. In order to accept the yoke of Torah, one needs a lot of commitment and an ability to stick to the commitment through thick and thin. Such a commitment is much more difficult when there is no sense of connection to previous generations.

Equally beneficial for ensuring that we stay in line is one's sense of obligation towards the honor of one's family. This double sense of

---

65   *Yalkut Shimoni, Remez* 684.
66   *Bamidbar* 1:3.

connection and obligation can help one stick through the commitment even when the going gets rough. Thus, only a nation with a clear pedigree and an awareness of family lineage was the best choice to be the recipients of the Torah.

LIFE LESSON

How can we ensure that our kids stay on the right path?

That's a really good question!

There are so many teens at risk nowadays; the numbers are simply staggering. We're terrified that our kids will join the sad statistics. We are busy double guessing our actions and worrying whether we're causing our kids to be turned off.

A good question deserves a good answer. But who has the answer? Who has the solution for this worrisome phenomenon?

While a solution is still desperately called for, there is a pretty potent antidote. It's deeply rooted in Eastern medicine and it's known as family. This homeopathic remedy can do wonders for warding off the at-risk epidemic. There are two components to this remedy:

- The anchor: This part consists of anchoring our families by forming an appreciation and a sense of connection to our ancestors.
- The bond: This part is about creating a healthy connection and a strong bond among the current family members.

So how does it work? It's really quite simple. By developing a historical connection to our ancestors we can help our children feel part of something great. There are many exciting ways through which we could accomplish this:

- We can develop a family tree as far back as we know. This would afford us and our kids a strong visual and tangible connection to the past.
- Pictures from the past, if we have any, are another amazing connection.

- We can make it a habit to speak to our kids about the life of our ancestors. Any story of our ancestors or even a simple snippet of information that we share is another anchor to the past.

These anchors will help keep the ship stable in the stormy seas of our times.

The second part of the remedy is all about creating and maintaining a strong family bond. This bond is formed by a slow-working potion. It calls for lots of time and patience. The more we invest in it, the greater the chances of its success. So if we want it to work, let's give it our all! Let's make it a priority to invest as much time as possible in building and maintaining a strong connection with our kids. The more we'll invest, the greater the dividends will be!

Where do we find extra time to spare for all that? Really, there is no need to *spare* time for our kids. We need to *make* time for them! They are our most valuable asset! Let us not lose them through neglect! By spending lots of time with our kids we'll strengthen their bonds with the family and their sense of loyalty. This will in turn serve as a pillar of support when things start becoming shaky.

This remedy need not be used only when there has been exposure or any other form of risk. It's highly recommended for anyone interested in a wholesome family! In fact, it's now being prescribed even for very young kids!

While a strong family connection is not a cure-all, it can and will go a long way!

The stronger the cable connecting our children to the family, the greater the chances that it won't be severed.

PROCESS VS. PRODUCT

T ime: Forty to fifty years after the destruction of the second Beis Hamikdash

Setting: Land of Judea

Backdrop: Yerushalayim is in shambles. Its Jews have been scattered to all corners of the vast Roman Empire. In the other towns and cities throughout Judea, Jewish life has rebound under the guidance of the revered *Tana'im*. The newly appointed Roman governor can't stand seeing how the Jews are living in relative peace and he is seeking for ways to embitter their life.

Debating Parties: The great Torah scholar, Rabi Akiva vs. the vicious Roman governor, Turnus Rufus

Rabi Akiva is an unwilling participant in this debate. He is very well aware of just how consequential the outcome of the debate could be. Turnus Rufus, on the other hand, is very confident that he will win. He's already prepared a slew of anti-Jewish decrees to be issued; the debate is just a formality to serve as a justification for the decrees.

Turnus Rufus starts off the debate, "Whose actions are greater, those of G-d or those of man?"

The question seems innocent enough; it's been debated many times throughout history in a variety of contexts. Educational and psychological professionals have debated this issue in the context of nature vs. nurture. Genetic engineers have faced off green-peace activists on this issue in the context of genetically modified foods.

Rabi Akiva answers, "Man's actions are preferred over those of G-d. Just see for yourself: here's a stalk of wheat — G-d's creation, and a loaf of bread — man's creation. Would you prefer G-d's creation over that of man?"

Rabi Akiva knows that it isn't just his philosophical bent that has prompted Turnus Rufus to call for this debate. There is surely something much more sinister lurking in the shadows of this question. Rabi Akiva, therefore, offers his unorthodox response. Turnus Rufus is totally thrown off by this answer. He has built an elaborate scheme on the assumption that the pious Rabi Akiva would surely answer that Hashem's actions were the greatest and beyond reproach. But, alas, there is no arguing with Rabi Akiva's proof!

Turnus Rufus asks, "If G-d wants people to be circumcised, why aren't they born that way?"

It's now plainly obvious that this is an attack on the mitzvah of *milah*.

Rabi Akiva answers, "Hashem gave us the mitzvos for the sole purpose of purifying us."

Turnus Rufus is defeated again. He has more than met his match in Rabi Akiva. The decrees against *milah* would just have to be shelved for the time being.

TORAH LESSON

The Ohr HaChaim explains that the debate between Rabi Akiva and Turnus Rufus was about product (result) vs. process.[67] Turnus Rufus looked at the world through the Roman lens, where the main focus was on the end result. The process was seen as a mere means to get to the result.

Rabi Akiva countered with the Torah perspective, which places process over product. It's not merely the product of the mitzvah that Hashem desires. He designed the mitzvos and commanded us to perform them as a way to provide us with the process that would serve to purify and elevate us!

LIFE LESSON

The main thing is the effort, or so we tell our children. But, do we really believe so?

Don't we want our kids to get straight A's?

Don't we hope that our kids will be at, or near, the top of their class?

True, when our kids bring home less than perfect report cards, we often pretend not to notice the low grades. We might even tell them that we only care about the effort that they invest, and it could very well be true. But then at night we get a sudden case of insomnia, and we toss and turn in bed wondering why our kids are performing so poorly. Somehow, those reassurances that effort is all that counts — which we've used to comfort our brokenhearted children — don't seem to be working for us!

We have a tendency to agonize when our children are not among the better ones in their grade. The efforts that our children invested even

---

67   *Vayikra* 12:3.

for their mediocre grades are all but forgotten. In reality, we tend to place a strong emphasis on the results, the product. We want an excellent product, no strings attached!

In fact, the product is so important to us that many of us willingly do our kids' projects. Why else would we parents slave on those homework assignments and projects for hours, trying to make sure that they turn out perfectly?

When a class performance comes up, we're again involved. Some parents even put their pride aside and call the school administration to help them in the process of selecting their child for a main part. By observing us in action, our children are absorbing the lesson that their efforts, and, by extension their unique personalities, don't really count so much. Instead, life is mainly about end results and, hopefully, stardom.

In real life, very few who aim for the stars actually reach them; most get lost in space! We run a great risk by trying to catapult our kids to the stars. They might feel we don't value them unless they're on top. When that proves to be too difficult, they might just give up and let go all the way, losing themselves in space.

We would do ourselves and our children a great service by learning to sincerely appreciate them for who they are and not only for what they produce. We would then be able to appreciate their unique challenges and personal victories. They will come to mean much more to us than the grade on the report card or test paper. They'll know that we really don't care what they got — we care mainly how they got it!

Let's think about it. By focusing on the product, the result, we're showing our children that they're only worth as much as their product is worth, which is not very encouraging. However, when we focus on the process, our children learn that they are unique and worthwhile individuals. The choice is ours!

Furthermore, even in the materialistic world, the process very often determines the quality and value of a product. Let's just think in terms of a unique masterpiece versus a Chinese, mass-produced copy. Which one would we perceive as more valuable?

Let's treat our children as unique masterpieces and we'll have more appreciation for the process.

The value of our kids' accomplishments is measured by the uniqueness of the process, not the end result!

KIDS ARE NOT PROPS!

R abbi and Mrs. Gutman were the perfect couple. They were both top of their class, real catches. When they caught each other, the *shidduch* was considered a no-brainer; the best boy with the best girl. They themselves also believed that they had indeed deserved — and received — the best. Both instinctively knew that everyone would be watching them and they were committed to live up to everyone's high expectations. Theirs would be a family for everyone to envy!

For every decision the couple made, they took into consideration the impression it would make. Rabbi Gutman joined the *kollel* he knew people of his caliber were expected to join. Mrs. Gutman chose a career path that would wow anyone who heard of it. It didn't really matter that she had no true interest in that field; after all, she owed it to all the people who had always told her that she was a cut above!

She couldn't let them down by choosing a not-so-glamorous career, even if it was one she truly enjoyed.

When the perfect little Gutmans put in their appearance, they were quickly inducted into the family business. They were dressed just so and were trained to always be on their best behavior. The extracurricular activities the kids participated in and the friends they associated with were all carefully regulated by their parents to ensure that it fit in well with the greater scheme.

TORAH LESSON

Lavan was the undisputed master of deceitfulness. His words and actions were generally driven by underhanded and perverted intentions. Yaakov gracefully weathered the sudden jolts, changes of beat, and unanticipated twists in the relationship with his father-in-law. Anticipating Lavan's moves, Yaakov tried to stay one step ahead of him. However, there was one exception where it seemed that Lavan had actually gotten the better of Yaakov: when he substituted Leah for Rachel.

True, Yaakov was strong worded with his reproach, but why didn't he just teach Lavan a lesson by sending Leah back? He had every right to do so. The Ohr HaChaim explains that, hurt as Yaakov was from this deception, he was determined to keep Leah as his wife.[68] He felt it was morally unbecoming to send her back. He thus devised a new plan to also marry Rachel.

While Lavan was perfectly at peace using his own daughters as props in his scheming plots, Yaakov was ready to endure an unfair additional seven years of backbreaking labor in order not hurt Leah, herself a victim of her father's cruelty.

LIFE LESSON

We would do anything for our kids, wouldn't we?

---

68   *Bereishis* 29:25.

Even when their wants and needs subtly clash with our broader picture of our family?

Without even realizing, we sometimes view ourselves as performing artists; the world is our stage and all of humanity is our audience. We work hard to perfect our act and we create elaborate backdrops to enhance our performance. We sometimes assess things according to their usefulness as props in our act. At times, we even choose which groups and organizations to associate with as part of the act.

Our kids are often inducted to play a vital part of our performance. We view them as extensions and representations of ourselves. (They are usually compliant; at least up to a certain age.) Possibly without our even being fully aware of it, there are things we do to our children or demand of them to enhance our image. This could manifest itself in the clothing we get them, the friendships we encourage, the standards we set for them, or the camps we send them to.

It's comical how we don't realize that others we encounter may similarly be in the midst of a performance. They too believe that they are performers on the world stage. They too view us as members of their audience! When we engage them socially, we try to put on an act in order to impress them, and when they respond, they are engaged in their very own act to impress us!

And yet, humorous as it is, there aren't enough neutral bystanders to appreciate the joke; many bystanders too are engaged in their very own acts! At times, we pretty much resemble a kindergarten play where everyone is an actor and there's no audience. Yes, of course we've become better actors over the years. Our performance has gained a level of sophistication, no arguing with that, but our mindset may have remained pretty much the same as in kindergarten. Some of us still believe that there is no one like us and we still try to impress everyone. How impressive!

Our performance is oftentimes so good that we ourselves get fooled by it! We become the unsuspecting victims of identity theft, as we lose our true identity and we start believing in our act. We then run the risk of losing touch with reality and not being able to relate enough to our kids' true needs.

- When our daughter doesn't want to wear a certain item of clothing that we bought, we could find it difficult to grant legitimacy to her opinion.
- When our son has a different opinion about which yeshiva to attend, we might perceive him as shallow, or too easily influenced by his peers.

When we find ourselves incessantly at odds with our children, it's time for us to pause and reflect. We ought to ask ourselves, "Are we truly looking out for the best interests of our children, or are we in the process of sculpting props?"

Rather than trying our hand at sculpting ourselves and our children, and becoming frustrated when it doesn't work so well, let's get in touch with our true selves. We might just be in for a pleasant surprise. We'll realize that our organic selves are even more appetizing than the processed and genetically modified version we've worked so hard to create!

Additionally, once we learn to appreciate our natural selves, we'll be able to release our children from their bondage as props. They will then be able flourish as beautiful individuals. It will open the gates of opportunity for our children to tap into their true potential. Being real won't always enhance our image, but it will surely enhance our lives!

Let's not educate our children so the neighbors will be impressed. Let's allow them to be unique and original.

SPEAK MY LANGUAGE PLEASE!

Говорят на моем языке пожалуйста!

At age sixteen, Chesky couldn't help feeling distanced from Yiddishkeit. He saw religion as a bunch of restrictions and limitations. He'd had his fill of hearing his father's threats of being consumed by the eternal fires of Gehinnom. When Chesky was younger, he actually had nightmares of black, frightening angels.

In Chesky's family, there was no joy in Yiddishkeit. Father would constantly remind the kids that keeping Torah and mitzvos was not about enjoyment. Rather, it was all about restrictions in order to be saved from the eternal fire and their father's wrath. The atmosphere at home was generally depressing.

To be fair, Chesky's father did tell his kids about the reward in the next world. He told them how good the mitzvos were, but it was all lip service; he didn't live it!

By the time Chesky was in his teens, he'd had enough. He craved a sense of satisfaction; he was starved for some joy in life. The lures of the street winked conspiratorially at Chesky. He had to resist the very real temptations of the modern world with the abstract idea of rewards awaiting him after his death. How unbalanced! As for his fear of Gehinnom, that had long worn off.

At the brink of the abyss, Chesky luckily met up with a fine Yid who opened up to him the beauty and fulfillment of a religious life. Chesky was attracted to this new language, it spoke to him. Suddenly, it wasn't primarily about restrictions anymore, it wasn't only about rewards after death.

Torah was about the joy of living a meaningful life, about enjoying every opportunity to be connected to something so great. He felt a connection to his loving Father and he wanted to safeguard that connection. It wasn't only about rewards in the next world. Life itself was rewarding. How satisfying and fulfilling!

TORAH LESSON

When Moshe Rabbeinu urged Bnei Yisrael to keep the Torah, he presented it to them as choosing between life and death, blessing and curse. The Ohr HaChaim explains that Moshe wasn't merely indulging in the use of euphemisms when he used those two sets of apparently repetitive terms.[69] They are reference to two very different constructs. With life and death, Moshe indicated the tangible benefits versus the negative consequences one would experience in the physical world. With the blessing and curse he hinted to the reward versus punishment in the next world.

---

69 *Devarim* 30:19.

Moshe asked Bnei Yisrael to choose life, the physical and tangible good. Moshe knew that by focusing on the tangible benefits of keeping the Torah, it would be easier for the people to swing their hearts in the right direction. After all, physical pleasure is the language of our hearts.

LIFE LESSON

Who doesn't want good kids?

We work so hard and we invest so much in our kids in order for them to grow into upstanding, fine Yidden. We teach them about the next world, we implant into their very conscious the concept of reward and punishment. We tell them all about the great pleasures of Gan Eden that'll await them for keeping the Torah. They also learn about the punishments for those who transgress the Torah. We want our kids to have a very real awareness of and appreciation for the next world. We want them to be excited about the eternal reward for their mitzvos.

All of the above is most definitely true; it's of utmost importance to teach all that to our children, and then some. Without a strong conscious awareness of the next world, there is little chance to remain steadfast in one's belief and pursuit of Torah and mitzvos. And yet, it might just not be enough!

When a very tangible temptation smacks our children in the face, the promise of reward in the next world might not be convincing enough. The pleasure feels so real, it entices and it calls, it pulls like a powerful magnet. The knowledge of an eventual spiritual reward doesn't speak to the heart, while temptations do. They're simply no match!

In fact, the mere act of spending time in our physical world pushes the awareness of the next world to the background. Therefore, it's imperative that we impart to our children — and to the child within us — that living a religious life is great and rewarding even in a physical sense.

We can create an air of excitement and joy in keeping the Torah. Our calendar is full of color; there's always some special day lurking right around the corner. These are all great opportunities to have fun and enjoy positive family time. Although tension and friction often find their way into these days, we could make a conscious effort to keep them out of the way. Anything associated with Yiddishkeit should be positively oriented. By doing so, we'll be communicating with the heart in its own language!

Additionally, we need not feel self-conscious or apologetic about our elevated status as religious people. It's okay to instill in our kids an inner joy for simply being a religious Jew. We could point out to our children how the materialism of Western society has imploded upon itself, how people are starved for some meaning in life. Note how even the best fed and materially successful people are going nuts from the lack of meaning and purpose in their life. Spirituality in its various twisted forms has become a multi-billion dollar industry as desperate people are eagerly lapping up any semblance of a higher calling.

We owe it to our progeny to impart in them a sense of joy and privilege for having the opportunity to lead a meaningful and quality life.

Make Torah life fun and enjoyable. That is the language of the heart!

TACKLE REBELLION
IN ITS INFANCY

Everyone knows that the American colonies rebelled because they wanted independence and the right for self-governance, right? Wrong!

In the decade leading up to the revolution, Great Britain started tightening its grip over the colonies through new laws and acts. The colonists, viewing themselves as proud Englishmen, expected to be treated as equals to their counterparts in England. They believed it within their rights to be represented in the British Parliament. All they wanted was to have a say in the making of the laws that would affect them.

The arrogant British ignored the (very reasonable) arguments of the colonists. Instead, they did just the opposite. They went on to enact highly unpopular laws known as the Sugar Act, Currency Act, Quartering Act, and Stamp Act, which placed more and more limitations on the colonists' lives. This understandably further enraged the colonists. Parliament continued to ignore the pleas and arguments coming from the colonies. The colonists went on to beseech King George III to intervene on their behalf. In response, the king labeled them as rebels.

Matters continued to deteriorate, and the relationship with England turned ever sourer. The colonists decided, as a final act of loyalty, to live up to the title that the king had graciously bestowed upon them, and the flag of rebellion was raised. The rest is history.

TORAH LESSON

Rashi quotes the Midrash that the underlying reason for Korach's rebellion was his jealousy of Elitzafan ben Uziel.[70] Korach believed that he should have been appointed as *nasi* of *bnei Kehas* rather than Elitzafan. Driven by this jealousy, he built up a whole case against Moshe and incited a general rebellion.

The Ohr HaChaim points out how all of Korach's arguments were in support of his original grievance against the appointment of Elitzafan. He compiled an extensive list of apparent inconsistencies with Moshe's actions. Korach thus tried to prove that Moshe's actions were not by divine order, which is obviously always consistent. Hence, Moshe couldn't be trusted with the appointment of his brother Aharon either; it was all about personal favoritism and self-aggrandizement.

Moshe hoped to nip this rebellion in the bud. He responded to Korach's accusations by bowing before the assemblage and showing them that he considered himself a nonentity, that they were all greater than he. (His ego was not part of the equation). If it were up to Moshe, he would step down without a moment's hesitation. However, it wasn't up to him, as all appointments came directly from Hashem. Hashem's commands are non-negotiable. Moshe, therefore, warned Korach that he was rebelling against Hashem and not Moshe.

LIFE LESSON

What's a synonym for adolescence?

It may very well be rebellion. It's almost expected of teenagers to rebel; it's part of their rite of passage. While our adolescents experience their identity crisis, the whole house goes into crisis mode. The once quiet home becomes a war zone, and there is no knowing when and where the next battle will break out. We feel under attack in our very own territory!

Our natural instinct is to go on the defensive. When our teens start voicing their grievances, we have a tendency to interpret it as rebellion. We then dig in and become tougher and more entrenched. Our children very often misinterpret this as proof that no one understands them or cares for their pain. This, in turn, stokes the flames of rebellion. When we continue reacting by digging in even deeper, they become convinced that we don't care for them. Before long, there's a massive war. Our outdated weapons and warfare strategies are seldom a match for our kids' modern and up-to-date weapons and newer tricks.

If you have an adventurous streak and enjoy the thrill of living in a war zone, this may be just fine.

However, for the faint of heart among us, let's try to explore some alternatives.

How can we nip the rebellion in the bud?

How can we ensure that our adolescents' grievances don't turn into full-blown rebellions that will destroy us, them, and the whole family in the process?

Let's call for a short armistice and survey the battlefield.

What is rebellion all about? Rebellion is generally a result of a buildup of intense hurt that had no other escape route. It just kept on growing and growing until it burst forth as a powerful and destructive force. Seldom is rebellion the first choice! Let's think about it: no one, child or adult, wants to venture off into unfamiliar territory unless the current situation feels unbearable. So how can we create an escape route for our children's hurt and ensure that it doesn't build up? How do we know when our children are hurting inside?

To be sure, we can't always know. Still, often we can. Very often, our children will throw hints at us, verbal or nonverbal, that they're sad and hurting inside. It's up to us to pick up on those hints. When we ignore those hints, our children might get the sense that their feelings are not valued. They then convince themselves that we don't really care so much about them. This belief tends to be extremely painful for our teens; their young minds have a hard time processing this pain! Thus, they give vent to their hurt through rebellion.

Experts in the trenches say that the greatest pain of abuse is not necessarily the abuse itself. It's when the child opens up to a trusted authority figure and he is not taken seriously, or worse, he is mocked. This has been termed secondary abuse. This secondary abuse is more traumatic to the child than the actual abuse!

Once a rebellion has become full-blown, it's very difficult to squelch it. By then, it feeds off itself as the teenagers get a perverted sense of satisfaction and fulfillment from the very acts of rebellion. It would take a lot to deal with it then.

Our best bet would therefore be to start tuning in to our children and to detect those early signs of pain. Let's not delude ourselves into believing that the pain will simply disappear. It might, but it might not, and then we'll pay a steep price. The gamble of sitting back and waiting it out is too great; there is too much at stake!

We can help our child by trying to sincerely understand why and how they feel hurt. We can create a safe environment to discuss with them their hurt without being judgmental. Even when we believe and know that our teens are seeing the picture all wrong, we would still do well to refrain from being judgmental. We can accomplish this by focusing on their feelings, not on their behaviors. Where feelings are concerned, there is no right or wrong. If our children feel hurt, the pain is very real, even if it was based on an imagined insult.

This is not necessarily an instant cure. They might not even be open with us right away. They're adolescents after all!

But over time, once they're convinced that we're sincere and accepting of them, they'll usually open up. We are then in a position to correct things. Very often we'll need to make concessions and we might even need guidance on how to repair our relationship. No matter what we need to do, we can do it and it is well worth it. It'll surely be easier than allowing the hurt to ferment and explode. An ounce of prevention is worth more than any cure!

Let's remember that rebellion is not a judgment on our parenting capabilities. It's about our children feeling hurt.

Once we remove our egos from the picture, it'll be much easier for us to stay objective. Why waste effort on reacting to the act of rebellion? Let's work on repairing the cause and not the symptoms!

Inside every teenage rebel resides a hurting child.
Let's focus on the hurt, not the rebellion.

THE BENEFITS OF BRIBERY

Baruch F. wouldn't hear of it! It was bad enough that circumstances had dumped him in this yeshiva. He looked at all the *bachurim* as strange, and he had absolutely no interest in forming any alliance with those aliens! Baruch considered himself more progressive than the rest of the *bachurim*, who were of primitive stock. He was determined to remain aloof and to count the days until the end of the year when he'd switch to a yeshiva that was more to his liking.

His father was at a loss. He was aware that this yeshiva wasn't the best match for Baruch, but there was nothing he could do for the remainder of the year, and he couldn't watch his son self-destruct. For lack of any other choice, Mr. F. promised Baruch that if he went along with the flow and mingled with the *bachurim*, he would receive an additional ten dollars weekly to spend on his growing *sefarim* collection. Father's money succeeded where his pleas had failed, and Baruch started integrating into the yeshiva.

Neither father nor son ever regretted this deal they struck. Baruch integrated beautifully into the yeshiva, and he ended up staying there throughout all the grades. Those primitive aliens now formed the core of his closest friends, and he couldn't have thought of a better yeshiva to attend.

TORAH LESSON

The Ohr HaChaim quotes a Midrash that when Moshe told Bnei Yisrael to circumcise themselves in Mitzrayim, many were just not ready to do it.[71] What did Hashem do? He brought forth an aroma from Gan Eden and perfumed Moshe's *korban Pesach*. When the people smelled this heavenly fragrance, they came begging Moshe for a piece. Moshe told them that they couldn't partake in the *korban* so long as they weren't circumcised. Upon hearing this, Bnei Yisrael immediately went ahead and had themselves circumcised.

It sounds incredible that Bnei Yisrael didn't jump at the command of Hashem. But it seems that some of them perceived circumcision as just too much. Hashem used the heavenly aroma as a form of bribery in order to motivate them.

LIFE LESSON

Which debilitating disorder do we collectively suffer from?

It's a disorder known by its professional name: CFAD. This condition usually sets in during early adulthood, especially once we start having children. It's a chronic condition that continues its progression throughout our lives. There are no available remedies or cures for this condition as of yet. The condition is also known as Childhood Feelings Amnesia Disorder.

---

71   *Shemos* 12:43.

In other words, we tend to forget how we felt as children when we believed we had been mistreated by the adults in our life. Due to this amnesia, we very often go ahead and do those very things we had promised ourselves not to do to our children!

This condition affects us in many ways. For example, we will often make demands and requests of our children that might be very difficult for them. Now, there is nothing wrong with this in and of itself. The issue arises when we are unable to connect with how our children feel about the difficult task. We simply can't understand why they're so reluctant to do what we asked of them. How can they ignore their parents' request and demand? There is a disconnect in our minds between the difficulty of the said request and our child's reluctance to do it, all due to this debilitating amnesia!

When we see our children stall, we oftentimes simply go ahead and repeat ourselves. When that doesn't bring us the desired results, we apply some more pressure and tell them yet again. This cycle can go on and on to infinity. Nothing really changes from one round to the next besides for our frustration levels, which keep on multiplying steadily. Einstein is credited for saying, "Insanity is doing the same thing over and over again and expecting different results."

Of course, there may be times when, by simply applying enough pressure, we would actually get our way. However, very often other methods are called for. This is especially true when we're asking of our children to do something difficult. Whether it's something truly difficult or just difficult for this child doesn't matter, as long as they perceive it as difficult.

We have a real problem because, as of yet, there is no proven cure for the CFAD condition, and it can get in the way of our relating to our children. The good news is that even if we can't treat the condition, there are many successful methods for getting around it. There is no need for us to revert to our childhood memories in order to help our children get past their impasse.

Even without fully understanding what's going through our children's minds, we could take note of the fact that things are just not working out as we've hoped. We can then go ahead and employ a well used adult trick known as bribery. Research has shown that it works on children just as well as on adults.

It's important to remember that bribery is a dish that is best enjoyed when doled out sparingly. Only when something proves to be really difficult, or when we feel we have no other option, should we use it. When we use too much of it, bribery magically morphs into payment, and payment has to be doled out more often and in greater quantities, and it's not nearly as potent as bribery. So let's stick to the golden rule of moderation.

Sometimes, money talks.

PARENTING IS NO CHILD'S PLAY!

Sruli, eleven, had his parents terrified of him. He knew how to play them like an expert circus master. Sruli had figured out how to make his parents jump at his requests and how to coax them into performing the most difficult moves. There was no question about it — Sruli was king in his house.

His parents did occasionally try to regain control by disciplining him. However, Sruli was way past that stage, and he knew exactly how to react to punishment. He would start howling that he hated his house and his parents. His parents would get all unhinged upon hearing this. They would come running, full of regret, trying to comfort him. Sruli would first let them stew in their regret, and then he would make a show of turning away from the parent who punished him and only accept the apologies of the other parent.

Eventually, Sruli's parents learned that if they were to punish him, he would start liking the other parent better and they would fall out of favor. This created a situation where both parents refrained from punishing Sruli and only tried to appease him all the time. Hence, the rule of King Sruli I was proclaimed.

TORAH LESSON

After Bnei Yisrael passed through the split sea, Hashem told Moshe to stretch out his hand over the sea and the waters would return upon the Egyptians on their chariots and on their riders. Why did Hashem ask Moshe to signal to the water to return to its normal flow? After all, it had only altered its course for the sake of Bnei Yisrael. Once they were all out of the water, there was no reason for the water to remain split! It should have returned automatically without the need for a second instruction.

The Ohr HaChaim answers that Hashem wanted the water to resume its flow specifically through an act of Moshe.[72] He was the one who disrupted its flow, so he would be the one to make it resume.

LIFE LESSON

What's parenting all about?

That surely is one tricky and sticky question! Parenting theories and models abound, and new ones are created all the time. So we'll try to focus on just one issue of parenting that tends to cross theory lines as it makes its appearance in many a household.

Dare we make a claim that, at times, some game playing finds its way into parenting? We're not talking about the games we parents play with our children. Rather, it's about subtle intra-spousal parenting games

---

72   *Shemos* 14:26.

that we sometimes play. So let's examine some of those games and their playing rules.

Of course, we stand united with our spouses in our *chinuch* approach. We know full well that for any approach in *chinuch* to be effective, it needs to be supported by both parents. So we cooperate with each other and we make joint decisions on which methods to use. And yet, with all the teamwork, there could develop a silent competition between us and our spouses. Even if we dare not admit it, we parents pine for our children's fullest love. If we believe that our children feel closer to their other parent, we might start experiencing this funny feeling which could be mistaken for something akin to jealousy.

So in order to rid ourselves of this unwanted funny feeling, we occasionally turn to game playing. Here, ping-pong is the game of choice. Whenever the need arises to discipline a child, we parents start playing ping-pong with each other. We each try to throw the ball at the other and have him/her do the disciplining. We believe that our spouse will find it easier to absorb the negativity caused by the disciplining.

Once the disciplining is taken care of, it's time for the parental racing session to begin. We try to outrun each other in our efforts to appease the disciplined child. It's a kind of good-cop bad-cop game. Of course, we never intend to paint our spouse as being the bad one or anything even remotely similar. We simply try to stay in the good graces of our children. The fact that our spouse might now be viewed as the bad one is an unintentional side effect.

Games are great to use in parenting and marriage. However, that's only in regards to games that we play *with* each other, not *at* each other! After all, we're all loving parents and not cops. Why should we even try to be the good cop? The best cop is not nearly as good as a parent, even as the parent who does the punishing!

Additionally, our kids are quick to pick up on the rules of the games and they easily become the uninvited players. Once our kids enter the game, they play it against both parents and then both parents end up as losers. More still, even our kids end up losing out because it's vital for their healthy development to have solid parents who have the confidence to say no and discipline when necessary.

So let's forget about the good-cop bad-cop game. Rather, let's be game in parenting our kids the right way. Let's learn to really work together with our spouses to accomplish what's truly best for our children. Our children will like us and appreciate us best when they feel that we really stand united and that we both love them equally.

We could accomplish this by establishing that the parent doing the disciplining should be the very one to comfort the child afterwards. It will provide our children with the very reassuring feeling that we still like them even though we punished them. It will also even out our parenting with no one parent being the good one or the bad one. We'll each have both hats and don them as needed. It'll be a game changer!

United we stand; divided we fall.

THE COOL THING
ABOUT CHINUCH

D uring the mid-sixteenth century, the pope expelled all Jews from the territories under his sovereignty. (For many centuries the popes ruled over large regions in central Italy known collectively as the Papal States). Lost and forlorn with nowhere to turn, the Jews found a savior in the figure of Guido Ubaldo da Montefeltro, Duke of Urbino (a region in Italy). He offered them asylum in his territories, especially in the city of Pesaro. The duke appeared as an angel of rescue amidst the darkness and confusion of the expulsion.

In truth, the duke was no special Jew-lover; he had only his personal interests in mind. He hoped that the refugees would develop the port of Pesaro and thus attract the Jewish merchant ships. But why should we care about the duke's intentions and that he only had his personal interests in mind?

The new settlers were quick to learn that intentions do matter, and they matter big-time. Much as they tried, the Jewish settlers at Pesaro could not divert the Jewish merchant ships to the new port of Pesaro. A few short years later, when a disappointed duke realized that his dreams hadn't materialized, he was quick to dispose of his Jewish subjects.

TORAH LESSON

The Rambam and Raavad disagree over why Hashem will punish the nations who oppressed the Yidden. After all, are they not fulfilling Hashem's will by inflicting suffering upon us in exile?

The Rambam claims that our oppressors will have to give an accounting for every bit of suffering that they caused us.[73] He explains that Hashem didn't designate any specific nation as our tormentors. Consequently, the nations who volunteered their services did so out of their intense hatred towards us. No lofty intentions there.

The Raavad says they will, indeed, only be held accountable for the extras, for tormenting us considerably more than Hashem had decreed.[74]

The Ohr HaChaim takes the Rambam's reasoning a step further and he explains that the extras are actually proof for the whole thing.[75] Had the motivation of the nations been only to fulfill Hashem's wish, they would have kept our suffering to a minimum. Thus, judging from their zealous fervor and how they surpassed any obligation to make us suffer, we can deduce that it stemmed purely from their contempt at our keeping the mitzvos.

So we see that not only does intention matter, it can actually change the whole picture!

---

73   *Mishneh Torah, Hilchos Teshuvah* 6:5.
74   Ibid.
75   *Vayikra* 6:2.

LIFE LESSON

We can't let our kids get away with everything, right?

We suddenly feel hot and sweaty and our heartbeat is racing. Our kid has just committed another one of his follies. How many times have we told him to stop misbehaving?! How dare he disobey again? Doesn't he realize that he's making our hairs turn gray?

We feel we have no choice but to teach him a lesson he'll remember. We, as his parents, have the responsibility to be *mechanech* him and ensure that he grows to be a decent human being!

After we've subjected our child to a lengthy lecture about his continuous misbehavior and we've imposed on him some tough consequences, our heart rate slowly goes back to normal. At times, we're gripped with uncertainty and guilt and we could question whether we're being too harsh. But we feel that even if we occasionally get really angry, it's still important for us to be *mechanech* our children.

Is it really *chinuch* we're practicing? At that moment of anger we lose our ability to think rationally. When that happens, chances are our *chinuch* obligation is not the primary driving force behind our actions. It's more likely that we become furious and frustrated as we get flooded with feelings of helplessness in the face of our child's undeveloped listening skills. We might even see his misbehavior as some sort of indicator of our own ineptitude as parents. And that's just too much for us to put up with! Thus, our reaction might end up being more about our subconscious need to prove we're in control and less about the necessary *chinuch* measure.

So what are we supposed to do to prevent this from happening?

Well, for starters, not much. When we start feeling hot due to our children's misbehavior, it should serve as a warning sign that we're leaving *chinuch* territory. *Chinuch* does not taste good when served hot! We would do well for ourselves and our children to first cool down! There's no need for us to join our heartbeat's race.

Once we've cooled down, we'd be in a much better position to evaluate the incident and decide whether our intervention is called for. Even when we do deem it necessary to punish or offer a consequence, when we're cool and rational the punishment will be much more in line with the actual offense.

What difference does it really make, you may ask. The main thing is for our children to know that they're being held accountable for their misdeeds. So what if we lose ourselves once in a while? We surely can't always wait until we calm down and risk letting our children get away with their misbehavior! It will harm their *chinuch*.

In truth, while there is a possibility that we'll miss the opportunity to discipline and our child might then repeat his offense, it will do much less damage than our reacting in anger. We need not worry that we'll be missing out on a *chinuch* opportunity, as no *chinuch* will be taking place anyway — guaranteed.

When our heat goes up, our ability to be mechanech goes down.

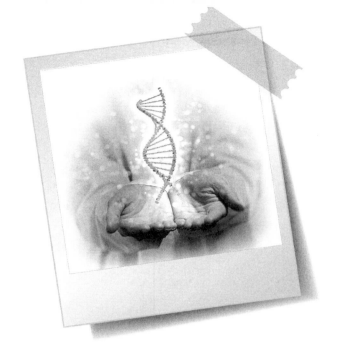

CRACKING THE GENETIC CODE

I n its early days of statehood, Israel was struggling with severe food shortages and austere rationing. The grocery stores had very little to offer and they were not permitted to give anyone more than what was indicated on his or her ration card.

One day, Cabinet Minister D. wanted to throw a nice party. Mrs. D. headed out to the black market where one could purchase decent food — for the right price. In order to cover up her actions, Mrs. D. took along a baby stroller and blanket in order to hide the food she would buy. Alas, the only food she was able to obtain was a cute little piglet. She carefully placed the piglet in the stroller, covered it up with the blanket, and quickly headed for home.

On her way, she had the bad luck of bumping into Mrs. Shalev, her neighbor. Mrs. Shalev eyed the stroller inquisitively and asked Mrs. D. whom she was pushing. Mrs. D. answered that she was taking her grandson for a walk. When Mrs. Shalev wanted to have a peek at him, the worried grandmother was quick to say that the baby was sleeping and it was preferable not to disturb him. However, disregarding the grandmother's pleas, Mrs. Shalev pulled off the blanket to catch a glimpse of the minister's sweet grandson. Upon seeing the "little one" she exclaimed in amazement, "Wow, he looks just like his grandfather!"

I guess there is something to this gene thing after all!

TORAH LESSON

Hashem told Avraham to leave his homeland and set out to the land He would show him. Hashem told him, "Leave your country, your birthplace, and your father's house."[76] The Ohr HaChaim asks, what was the point of Hashem detailing to him to leave his birthplace and his father's house? When Avraham would leave his country, wouldn't he obviously also leave his birthplace and father's house?

He explains that Hashem was referring to the levels of connection and emotional pain involved in the separation from those places. The levels from lowest to highest are:

Country of origin — It's part of a person's identity and he feels a connection to it, but it's not a very strong one; he could disassociate quite easily.

Hometown/birthplace — The attachment is much stronger and the separation anxiety is greater.

Close family — Here the bond is on a completely different level. Family is part of one's very essence! Even more than one is part of his family, his family is part of him. Most of a person's personality traits, behaviors, and makeup are rooted in his parents and family; they are part of his genetic code. Severing all of those chords is akin to giving up

---

76   *Bereishis* 12:1.

one's very personality! It calls for superhuman emotional strength to accomplish this.

Hashem wanted to reward Avraham for the emotional pain he would endure for the sake of Hashem's command.

Hashem started from the lowest level of pain (leaving his country) and eventually moved on to the greatest level, namely leaving his father's home.

There is something to this gene thing after all!

LIFE LESSON

Who doesn't want great kids?

We all want great kids! We desperately want our kids to be happy and successful in life. We are greatly bothered when we notice negative traits and harmful tendencies in our children. We try to do whatever is in our power as parents to set them straight, and we go to great lengths to accomplish that.

However, if we care to take note, we might realize that it's often more than just about trying to help our kids. There are some traits and shortcomings in our children that don't just bother us — they drive us crazy! Whenever we come across those weaknesses, we tend to feel like we were rubbed raw, which could cause us to respond in an exaggerated manner. Those are the issues we lash out about time and again.

It would be very interesting for us to take note of those very bothersome behaviors. Often, we'd realize that those irksome traits are the very same ones that we ourselves struggled — or are still struggling — with. When we see our own shortcomings reflected in our children, we tend to take it very hard. Without even realizing it, we might come down overly strong on our kids for those things.

In reality, we'd do well to realize that we're being unfair to our children. They didn't choose the traits they're struggling with; we bequeathed it to them together with their genetic makeup. More still, trying to force them out of those traits is akin to asking them to rewrite their DNA and to cut their ties with us, their parents. After all, it's from us that they've inherited them!

Looking at it from this vantage point, maybe we should take it out on ourselves for passing on to our kids such faulty traits? On second thought, are we possibly viewing our kids as our second chance? By lashing out at them do we hope to correct our own shortcomings?

Be it as it may, it's surely unfair to try to use our children as proxies to finish off our personal unfinished business. Our kids don't have to carry the brunt of our shortcomings! True, they have issues they need to work on, but so do we. Before we work on our children, let's work on ourselves!

As long as we ourselves are struggling with those very hardships, we obviously haven't yet figured out a way to rid ourselves of those problems. That being the case, how can we possibly have the proper approach to help our children overcome them?

Let's remember that our children are part of our identity, and yet, they are individual beings simultaneously. Instead of identifying their problems, let's identify with them and their struggles. Let's offer our children the same sensitivity and understanding of their shortcomings as we would offer ourselves.

There is something to this gene thing after all!

Our children are not our second chance. They are their very own first chance!

FRAGILE, HANDLE
WITH CARE!

T he war was raging; the battles were fierce. A hor-
rible show was being played out in the Pacific
theatre. A great many thousands had already been
killed and the calm waters were red with blood,
but there was no end in sight. The Japanese were determined
to fight on. The allied forces were demanding unconditional
surrender, but the Japanese wouldn't hear of it. The world
watched with terrified fascination as a new and frightening
bomb wiped out two cities. Everyone anticipated surrender,
but it didn't happen. The Japanese appeared indestructible,
and a full-blown invasion loomed inevitable.

The pressure on Japan increased from day to day, especially
with the opening of the Russian front. Yet there were still
some extreme factions in the military who wouldn't hear of

surrender. They only came around after the conditions for capitulation were amended, and the emperor was allowed to remain the figurehead of Japan, albeit stripped of his power and divinity. What was it about this seemingly minor change that helped those extreme factions change their minds?

The Japanese possessed a major source of power unmatched by Western military might: pride. The Japanese were fighting for their pride, and surrender just wasn't an option. Conventional warfare was powerless against this pride. By allowing the emperor to remain as their figurehead, their pride was somewhat salvaged. Hence, they were ready to open their eyes and acknowledge that it was high time they surrender.

TORAH LESSON

The Torah tells us that Yosef's brothers were guilt-ridden and full of remorse over what they had done to Yosef by selling him into slavery.[77] Chazal tell us that they were ready to go to great lengths to redeem him, and Yosef was well aware of that.[78] Yet, the Torah tells us, when Yosef revealed himself to his brothers, he begged them not to become enraged.[79] One would wonder where rage comes into the picture. Shouldn't the brothers have been ecstatic when Yosef revealed himself?

The Ohr HaChaim explains that while they were ready to do whatever possible to redeem him, they were very hard-hit when they saw him as viceroy. They were under the impression that they had taken every precaution to ensure that Yosef's dreams would never come to fruition. And now, the dreams' fulfillment stared them in the face. As powerful as the brothers' guilt and remorse may have been, it stood no chance against the tidal wave of destructive energy caused by their injured pride.

---

77   *Bereishis* 42:21.
78   *Bereishis Rabbah* 91:7.
79   *Bereishis* 45:5.

The only way Yosef was able to save the situation was by saving their pride. He helped his brothers recognize that everything was part of Hashem's greater plan, even their original hatred. This mitigated the blow and reconciled them with Yosef.

LIFE LESSON

What's the most destructive energy we know of?

It depends.

In the physical world, the fission of an atom releases megatons of destructive energy.

In the emotional world, the fission of our pride could prove to be equally destructive. It's liable to produce megatons of destructive energy. When internalized, this energy is likely to destroy our self-esteem and make us feel worthless. When externalized, it could create tidal waves of anger, rage, revenge, and destruction.

Unlike the atom, it doesn't take scientists to figure out how to bring about the fission of pride. Pride is generally vulnerable and open to attack and trampling. This is all the more true with kids' pride, which is extremely fragile!

Oftentimes, we're not even aware of how our words or actions end up injuring our children's pride. Our younger children usually internalize the injury and hurt, whereas our teens often externalize it by getting into fits of rage and indulging in other destructive behaviors. In fact, many times children both internalize and externalize their reaction, destroying themselves and their surroundings in the process.

So when our teen suddenly withdraws or explodes without any apparent reason, it's an alarm. It's warning us that a mishap has occurred at the nuclear reactor and our teen's pride had been injured. (This is not talking about the times when our kid throws a temper tantrum for persuasive purposes.)

To complicate matters, teens tend to have very complex prides. It's very inflated yet ultra fragile simultaneously! Anything and everything we say can be interpreted as an attack on their egos and might set off a full-blown and devastating nuclear reaction. They might react by sulking, throwing tantrums, and hurtling accusations at us. And try as we might, we can't speak to them. Reason becomes an unwelcome intruder, and they remain "Closed for Destruction" until further notice.

We, in turn, become defensive and claim that we've said nothing wrong! But, alas, the more we go on the defense justifying ourselves, the more our kids take offense. We watch forlornly as our teens retreat behind a wall of adolescent self-righteous mistrust and feelings of victimization.

We stare at that wall and we get the feeling that our kids are off-limits; we can't tell them anything anymore! We blame them for misinterpreting everything we say. They, in turn, blame us for being overbearing, out of touch, and out to get them. The more we dig into our respective trenches, the less chance we stand to straighten out the territory. Understandably, nobody stands to gain from this exchange of pain and mistrust!

So how can we prevent war from breaking out?

We could try to keep the area as clean of explosives as possible. We could start by taking note of what issues cause our teens to act up. We can then learn to modify our approach in a way that would not upset our teens' sensitive systems.

Let's also learn to feel our children's pain, frustration and hurt, even on issues that we disagree upon. Remember, it isn't easy being a teen! We could work on truly understanding their concerns and empathizing with their feelings, even while disagreeing with their requests. At times, it might even be beneficial to compromise.

We need not be afraid that by paying attention to their feelings we'll be condoning and encouraging inappropriate behavior. Nothing could be further from the truth, as understanding does not equal excusing!

In fact, the opposite is true! Our kids are often flustered themselves by their reactions and they can't even articulate what ticked them off. Our show of understanding will help them gain a better understanding of themselves. It will also teach them such valuable life skills as healthy communication, empathy, negotiation, and compromise. Not such a bad deal, is it?

In addition to all these benefits, there is another great reason to try understanding our children and thus protecting their pride. Let's remember that pride could be an amazingly empowering emotion. It's worthwhile preserving our children's pride because it could help them accomplish great things when harnessed successfully.

Our children's pride can be one of their greatest assets in life. Let's build it, not break it!

HONOR YOUR WORD!

T he campaign was a brilliant one. Everyone was able to relate to the central campaign message of CHANGE!

Who wasn't hoping for change?

The economy was in shambles, the country was stuck in two drawn-out military campaigns, and the world at large was poking fun at the expense of the deflated giant. During the campaign, a great many promises were made in the name of change. So much hope was pinned on the optimistic message of change. There was going to be renewal across the board. The antiquated and cumbersome bureaucracy would be replaced with a better, more workable system. The government would create initiatives to offer everyone an equal chance. Amazing!

The candidate won. Now it was time to prove to the nation that they were right in placing their confidence in him. It was time to start implementing those changes he had promised.

The nation was holding its collective breath to see how things would play out and what those changes would look like. What did they get in return? Their candidate shared some very telling words, "We need to lower our expectations while keeping up our hopes." How devoid of commitment! How telling!

As one famous politician aptly put it, "I promised, but I never promised to keep my promises!"

TORAH LESSON

The Ohr HaChaim[80] quotes a Chazal stating, "The annulment of vows floats in the air."[81] This refers to the fact that there is no mention in the Torah that a sage can annul a vow; it is a *mesorah* of Chazal. Seldom, says the Ohr HaChaim, do we find that there should be absolutely no mention in the Torah of a mitzvah, and we would only know about it through *mesorah*. *Mesorah* usually only adds details to something already mentioned in the Torah. Why, indeed, did Hashem conceal this mitzvah?

He explains that Hashem didn't want it written for all to see that vows and promises could be annulled. This would cause people to take the matter lightly. Promises would become cheap. People would make vows without much thought, knowing that they could have their words cancelled whenever they fancied.

Hence, Hashem hid the laws of annulment and gave it over to the *gedolei Yisrael*. They possess the clarity to know and differentiate which vows can be invalidated. However, the masses will know only that they have to keep their word, no strings attached.

LIFE LESSON

What's cheap, really cheap?
Words are cheap!

---

80   *Bamidbar* 30:2.
81   *Chagigah* 10b.

Or, are they? In recent years, we've collectively become more politically savvy. Alongside this political suaveness, we have possibly learned from our elected politicians that we need not honor our word. At times, we make promises but we're not careful enough to remember them. We have compromised on the value of our words!

We parents find it very disconcerting when we catch our children distorting the truth. We all want our kids to grow up to be trustworthy adults. Yet are we really fully committed to the truth? We're surely not deceitful cheats, but perhaps we're not such guardians of the truth either. Somehow, words have become cheap and promises have lost some of their value. We take on commitments but we sometimes forget about them, we make deals and we don't always remember them.

We're good people. We surely have no intention to lie; we just don't give our words enough thought and we're not pressured enough to remember them. We have adopted a laid back attitude toward honoring our words. We have added a touch of flexibility to the truth so it can stretch and bend a little when necessary.

Additionally, we might not realize the effect and impact that our forgetfulness has on those around us. Let's take a step back and look at the broader picture.

Before sending out the invitations, the *baalei simchah* gave a lot of thought to whom to send dinner cards. On the one hand, every portion is an additional expense, but on the other hand, it's so beautiful to have lots of people at the *simchah*. It was exciting when people sent back their return cards stating that they'd attend. But at the *simchah* many guests failed to show up. The extra expense was incurred with nothing to show for it, all because people weren't careful enough to honor their word. Is it fair?

The yeshiva administration was very excited at the volume of ads the journal had generated. The hundreds of hours spent on the dinner and journal campaign were well worth it. The revenue they hoped it would generate would really come to good use. However, after the dust and glitter of the dinner settled, the administration was quick to learn that pledges and donations don't always go hand in hand. So much wasted time and energy and so many dashed hopes. Why?

We made deals with our kids and we had every intention of keeping them, but we forgot. Our kids were excited with the deal and they tried doing their part. They were waiting eagerly for us to keep our part of it, but we didn't because we forgot. They didn't feel comfortable reminding us about it. How do our kids feel about this?

Whether it's in our interactions with them or in our interactions with others, our kids tend to develop a sense of our value system. When our kids don't value their own words, they might just be proving to us that they are good learners; they've picked up on the (lack of) value we place on our own words.

Let's focus on raising the value of words in our families. Let our kids see that we take our words very seriously and they will usually follow suit.

Additionally, we'll be more respected in the eyes of our kids and those around us when they know that they can count on our honesty.

We ourselves determine the value of our words
according to how much value we attach to them!

COMPLIMENTS AND CRITICISM: NOT GOOD PARTNERS

The United Nations is hard at work. In its perpetual obsession with world peace, the refined diplomats can't sit by idly while human rights are being violated the world over. The aggressive Israeli occupiers are understandably highest on their list due to their torturing and slaughtering of innocent civilians. The UN is so worried about the sorry state of the beleaguered Palestinians that they've willingly turned a blind eye to all the real genocide and mass injustice happening anywhere else, especially among the Arabs themselves.

The Israeli government has tried pleading its case in front of the UN countless times. The Israeli argument is based on the skewed belief that a country is allowed the very basic sovereign right of protecting itself against terrorists who want nothing more than to destroy it. Understandably, every country could relate to this argument, and, as expected, everyone identifies and accepts the argument. However, there is always a "but." It goes something like this, "You surely have the right to protect yourself, but the battleground has to be more leveled," whatever that's supposed to mean.

The "but" serves very effectively as a magic erase button, which just erases everything that was said up until then. Furthermore, it serves to abort every attempt to offer any additional logical argument. How brilliantly simple and maliciously effective!

TORAH LESSON

The Torah relates how Rivka went home and showed off the gifts she received from Eliezer. "And to Rivka there was a brother and his name was Lavan, and Lavan ran to the man outside to the well."[82] The Ohr HaChaim brings to our attention that by righteous people the Torah writes the term "and his name was" preceding the actual name. By the wicked, however, the Torah would write the name first. Thus, he asks, the *pasuk* should have written, "and Lavan was his name." Why was the wicked Lavan deserving of righteous mention?

The Ohr HaChaim explains that when Lavan saw the gifts Rivka had received, he suspected some foul play, and he ran to righteously avenge his sister's compromised honor. Wicked as Lavan was, at that moment he acted meritoriously and Hashem doesn't withhold anyone's award. Hence, his wickedness notwithstanding, Lavan received this honorary mention as a reward for his good deed. There were no "buts" and no strings attached. His many misdeeds didn't overshadow or cancel out this good deed.

---

82   *Bereishis* 24:29-30.

LIFE LESSON

What's arguably the worst word in the English language?

No, it's not one of those terms thrown about during temper induced vocabulary contests. Neither is it one of those finer, more polished expressions used at bipartisan political mudslinging competitions. This terrible word is rather nondescript and low-profile. It conceals its toxic potency behind an innocent façade. It strikes its victims unawares and often leaves devastation in its wake.

And the word is . . . but!

Simple word, isn't it?

Actually, no. Not in the least bit! While it was originally designed as a low profile sentence enhancer, it has successfully been adapted as a very effective lethal tool. How is that so?

We've all heard and read our fair share of the importance of being complimentary and praising our kids. We've collectively internalized those messages. Compliments have become commonplace. However, there are times when our parental duty calls upon us to offer our kids some correctional feedback. We try to do it ever so gently, and in order to soften the blow, we often start out by complimenting our child. We then go on to add the "but" word followed by some correctional advice. It could sound something like this:

"Moishy, you're doing a great job in your learning and we really get good reports, but what about your *middos*? There is still some room for improvement there!"

We might have every intention of doing the right thing by complimenting generously, but in reality, we haven't complimented him at all! More still, we were actually critical and exceptionally hurtful. Why? Because "but" has the power to turn the first half of the sentence into an introduction for the latter part. The compliment actually makes the criticism all the more painful! It's could come across as saying, "Moishy, all of your learning is not worth as much so long as you don't correct your *middos*." Quite hurtful, isn't it?

We sometimes wonder why our children claim that we don't appreciate their efforts and we only focus on their wrongdoing. We tend to get unnerved by these accusations, as we have made it our business to compliment them generously. And even when we did feel the need to offer some correctional advice, we did it only after giving them a compliment. Why, then, do our kids have to twist things so out of perspective?

The answer might very well be that terrible word "but." (This is obviously besides for the times that their victim stance is merely part of some adolescence fad.)

How can we compliment and offer the necessary feedback without the "but"?

It is, in fact, pretty simple. Often, we can switch the "but" for another simple word: "and." It could go something like this, "Moishy, you're doing great with your learning and we really get good reports, and you have it within you to do great with your *middos* as well."

It looks like a mere play of semantics, and yet it makes a world of a difference. While "but" indicates a strong change of course and a departure from the previous track, "and" signifies a smooth continuum. Don't we all appreciate a smooth ride over a rugged one?

When we determine the need to offer correctional feedback, let's do it using the word "and." It'll really improve our correctional feedback skills, and it'll also improve our kids' acceptability skills.

Let's use compliments to praise our children, but
not as complements to our criticism!

MINIMIZE THE DAMAGE

The battles were fierce and unrelenting. Yudi, twenty-six and living at home, simply couldn't be woken up in the mornings. Much as his parents tried to wake him in time for *krias shema*, it was useless. They couldn't digest Yudi's laid-back attitude toward such basics as *krias shema* and davening. For hours on end every single morning, they would try every trick in the book and then some, but with no success. Blaring and vibrating alarm clocks, ringing phones, drenching the pillow, turning over the mattress, mother's desperate pleas — nothing seemed to work. Yudi would say "Yes, yes," but then drift right back into the world of nothingness. By mid-afternoon, Yudi would roll out of bed all refreshed and ready to tackle (and strangle) whatever time was left of the day.

Yudi was totally nonchalant about his sleeping habits. His mother, on the other hand, went nuts. His parents consulted *rabbanim* and experts and were told to let Yudi be. He was already an adult by all definitions; it was time for him to take responsibility for his actions. His parents were advised to desist from their waking ritual, as it accomplished nothing other than to alienate Yudi. They were even warned that their persistence might actually backfire, as it would deepen the rift between Yudi and them. The suggestion was good, the reasoning was great, but Yudi's parents refused to let go. They simply couldn't accept the idea that they should willingly allow Yudi to sleep to midday and to miss *krias shema* and davening.

TORAH LESSON

Hashem told Moshe, "Send for your sake *meraglim*." The Ohr HaChaim explains that the Bnei Yisrael requested from Moshe to send scouts to discover where the Canaanites where hiding their valuables.[83]

Moshe initially fell for their ploy and he asked Hashem for authorization. Hashem told Moshe that he could send for "his sake" — for what he believed their intentions to be. Hashem revealed to Moshe the true intentions of Bnei Yisrael, how they planned to misuse this mission. Hashem even showed Moshe the dire consequences of this act. Thus, the mission was doomed from the outset.

Why, then, didn't Hashem prevent it? Why didn't He tell Moshe to sternly warn Bnei Yisrael against sending the spies?

Furthermore, Hashem actually granted His consent, albeit with a warning attached. Why?

The answer is incredibly important for us. Hashem, in His infinite wisdom, knew that should He disallow it, the damage would be even greater! Misusing the power of their *bechirah*, they would descend to even lower depths. He knew that in the current situation

---

83 *Bamidbar* 13:2.

the best option was to give in to their demands, consequences notwithstanding.

It's what we would call minimizing the damage.

LIFE LESSON

What's the most difficult task entrusted to mankind?

Rocket science? True, it's complicated, but at least it's predictable. With some effort, it makes sense.

Raising teens? Now that is difficult! They are complicated, unpredictable, and they make absolutely no sense! There are so many rules to raising teens and so many exceptions to those rules; it's simply hard to recognize the rule from the exception!

So what are the rules and what are the exceptions?

Who knows? Every teenager comes with his/her own unpublished owner's manual! No two are alike!

There are, however, some generalizations we could explore for contemplative purposes only. For personal applications, please defer to the individualized owner's manual!

One important principle is stepping back and letting go. Providing our teens with some space and affording them the opportunity to make their own mistakes. It sounds so simple, but boy is it complicated! We've spent years standing by our children and pointing them in the right direction. Now that they've matured somewhat we feel we can finally have an intelligent conversation with our teens, that we can really explain and direct. Instead, we're told that it's time to start stepping back.

We might rightfully think that since they're at such a sensitive juncture in their lives, they so desperately need sensible guidance. We are there for them to happily provide all that. But, no. We have to give them space. Doesn't make too much sense, does it?

You can't teach an old dog new tricks, but we parents have to learn a whole repertoire of new tricks. Worst of all, we have to become great masters in the art of balancing. As we learn to walk the tightrope of parenting teens, we're faced with this delicate balancing act between being actively involved and letting go. If we're too strongly involved, our adolescents might view us as overbearing and then feel stifled. But if we let go, we're really doing our children a disservice since they're not mature enough to face a confusing world on their own. So how can we do it?

Who knows?

No delusions here. The letting go thing is not only about the at-risk population. In fact, every adolescent is unfortunately at risk to become an at-risk teenager. Sorry, no exceptions there. Too many formerly good kids were believed to be exceptions! There's a storm of destruction raging in the world, and it doesn't take all that much for an adolescent to find him/herself in the maelstrom.

Parenting adolescents is becoming more and more about gentle guidance and encouragement. We ought to invest a lot to learn and figure out when we need to stand on our principles and when to let go.

At times, we might bravely make concessions, sometimes even major ones. We go along with it outwardly, but resentment and self-doubt gnaw at our innards and give us no rest. It just feels all wrong! How can we allow our very own children to engage in self-destructive behaviors? We want to stop them! We desperately want to explain to them that their decisions will end up hurting them. True, we force ourselves to refrain from intervening, but our parental instincts are rubbed raw!

Yes, unfortunately there are times when we are powerless to prevent our children from hurting themselves. When they're determined to continue on their self-destructive path, we need to step back. We can't stop them, but we can try to minimize the damage. Oftentimes, this is accomplished precisely by actively allowing them space to experiment and learn from their mistakes. By giving our teens space, they will have less of an urge to rebel and to do things simply to spite us. It could even help them develop a healthy sense of self and a sense of responsibility.

So now that we don't have to stand on top of our teens so much, we have some extra time. We could utilize this time to develop a closer and more loving relationship with our maturing children. When the ground turns shaky, there is nothing more reassuring for adolescents than a solid parental relationship.

Also, even if it doesn't help our kids, it will help us conserve our sanity! This conserved sanity will come to good use!

The acts we do that totally go against our parental instincts are the ultimate examples of parental love.

Many times the best way to hold on is to let go!

MODEL FOR SUCCESS!

M r. Sappir used to say, "As my children started growing up, I decided that five minutes before they came home from *cheder* I would sit down and learn. I felt it was important for their *chinuch* that they see me learning. It would ignite in them a love for Torah and they would follow my example. I must have done something right because they did, indeed, follow my example. Five minutes before their children come home they too sit down to learn."

Mr. Gross was very into the *chinuch* of his kids and he went to great lengths for the sake of *chinuch*. Moishy, his seventeen year old, was always tense and on edge, and it disturbed Mr. Gross greatly. He wanted his son to learn how to relax and take things easy.

After all, Mr. Gross made it his business to be especially calm when his kids were around. By self-admission, he worked hard to portray an image of calmness for his kids. Why didn't Moishy take after him? Why was he always like a coiled spring?

In fact, Moishy *did* take after his father. All other times, when Mr. Gross was not next to his kids, he was tension incarnate. Spending any amount of time with him was a challenge. He was extremely tense and guarded, and every engagement with him was a tension inducing experience. One could literally feel the tension in the room when he was around. He was like a tinderbox.

It was a shame that Mr. Gross invested so much effort in modeling calm behavior to his kids. Somewhere between the modeling lessons his true nature leaked through — and that was what the kids picked up on.

TORAH LESSON

The Torah states, "A man his mother and father they should fear."[84] The Ohr HaChaim asks why the *pasuk* starts out in singular form — a man — and finishes with the plural — they should fear. He offers the following explanation. If a child observes his father behaving unbecomingly to his own father, the son too will have no respect. However, when one has the appropriate fear and respect for his parents, his own son will take heed and likewise fear and respect him. Thus, one person's observance of this mitzvah will result over time in many people observing it.

The son will learn all about fearing and respecting parents simply by observing his parents doing just that! No artificial modeling here, only the real stuff.

LIFE LESSON

How can we turn our kids into model children?

By modeling good behavior, of course! We live in a model-driven society where people strive to imitate models and copy role-models.

---

84   *Vayikra* 19:3.

We've been made to believe that the best way to impart desirable traits and practices to our children is by modeling those behaviors to them. *Chinuch* has surely become much more exciting now that it includes modeling and acting!

Like every good Jewish parent, we strive to see our children turn out great. We're ready to give it whatever it takes. So even though we've never graduated drama school, we throw ourselves completely into the modeling act. Even if we're not yet fully ready to personally take on certain behaviors, we would still love our kids to have them, so we try to model it for them. Easy, simple, and neat!

With this amazing modeling model, we basically create two sets of coexisting behaviors. There is the incredible *chinuch* modeling mode that we use whenever our children are around, and then there is the default mode where we allow our natural selves to come forth.

We invest so much thought and effort in trying to model desirable behaviors, we ought to stop for a moment and think. Do we really believe that our children are no more than modeling clay? Can our conscience allow us to accept that all it takes to impart desirable traits to our kids is some molding and modeling?

Acting surely has its virtues, especially in the entertainment arena, but not so much on the *chinuch* arena.

Why not?

Because it so happens to be that our children have extremely fine-tuned antennas that pick up the slightest inconsistencies in our behaviors. What we teach and model to our children is totally irrelevant if we don't truly embody it. Our true beliefs and feelings just leak out without us even realizing! And it's those inner messages that truly shape our kids. (Perhaps we could use the modeling clay to stop up those leaks.)

So if modeling appropriate behaviors accomplishes little, and our acting skills are lost on an unappreciative audience, are we just supposed give up? Should we just sit by and allow our kids to grow like untended weeds? Not necessarily. We can and we should teach the right behaviors. We just need to implement one small strategic change, namely first teaching *ourselves*.

Our focus should be on ourselves — that we should come to embody the traits and *middos* we want our kids to embody. Once they become part of our personality, our kids will pick up on it almost on their own. Very little instruction or modeling will be needed. Isn't that a great bargain? We'll get to improve two people for the price of one! Wow!

Of course, modeling does have its value. It's an accepted practice among sculptors to create a model before creating the actual sculpture. So too, we are oftentimes apprehensive about the new behaviors that we want to work on. We have a fear of the unknown. We can then use modeling to give us a feel and appreciation of the targeted behaviors. Those models can then help and guide us when we're actually sculpting our *middos* and behaviors. Then, our modeling mode and natural mode will become comfortably integrated into one entity.

We will feel better and more wholesome with only one set of behaviors. And our children will find it much easier to follow in our footsteps when there is only one set of footsteps.

Let's become better people. We deserve it! Our children deserve it!

If a behavior is worth modeling, it's worth being!

OUTSOURCING
A BAD IDEA

T he 1970's were tough years for Yidden living in Israel and elsewhere. The Palestinian Liberation Organization was a powerful, fierce, and sneaky terrorist organization. They carried out numerous terrorist attacks and hijackings and no Jew felt safe. The Palestinians where extremely proud of the PLO's accomplishments, and the organization gained more adherents with every atrocity they committed.

In their quest to weaken the PLO's influence, the Israeli government decided to make use of a proxy through which to strike the PLO. They assisted in the funding and strengthening of a competing Palestinian organization that was founded for humanitarian purposes. It was hoped that inner political bickering would help weaken the PLO.

The new organization was indeed a great success and it quickly gained many enthusiastic followers. They offered Arab-style humanitarian services.

The organization came to be known as . . . Hamas!

Need we say more?

History has a unique way of offering perspective.

TORAH LESSON

The Torah starts out the story of Moav hiring Bilam to curse Bnei Yisrael by telling us, "And Balak ben Tzipor [new king of Moav] saw all that Yisrael did to Emori. And Moav feared the nation [Yisrael]."[85] The Ohr HaChaim asks, Why does the Torah pin Moav's fear only on Balak and not, more generally, on the nation as a whole? Secondly, why does the Torah use the expression "Balak saw," and not that he heard?

The Ohr HaChaim explains that Balak was a great sorcerer. He used a bird for his sorcery. This is hinted at in his name — ben Tzipor, son of a bird. Through his sorcery, Balak was actually able to see the devastation that Bnei Yisrael had wrought upon Emori. Additionally, he also saw into the future that Moav had no reason to fear Bnei Yisrael, as they were commanded not to hurt Moav. Not so his own nation Midian. He saw that they had good reason to fear Bnei Yisrael. However, no one but Balak was privy to this information.

In an act of utter self-interest, Balak decided to cash in on Moav's panic in order to save his own homeland, Midian. Balak used Moav as a proxy to do all the dirty work against Bnei Yisrael. He figured Bnei Yisrael would be defenseless against them, as they were prohibited from hurting Moav. Midian will surely not be held accountable for Moav's misdeeds and Midian will thus be spared.

In the end, his plan backfired big-time. Not only did Balak gain nothing from trying to outsource the dirty work to Moav, he actually lost everything. He lost his kingship when Bilam revealed to Moav that they

85   *Bamidbar* 22:2.

had nothing to fear from Bnei Yisrael. He lost his daughter Kosvi when she behaved immorally as per Bilam's advice. And all of Midian was killed!

LIFE LESSON

How often do we use proxies in the *chinuch* of our children?

How many times do we outsource difficult parenting tasks?

Oh no, not us! We don't shy away from any parenting tasks, difficult as they may be, right?

But consider this:

Young kids are sometimes convinced to go to bed on time in order not to sleep outside with the cats.

They behave in the car because they don't want the police to come.

They obligingly come along with us on boring errands because staying home alone could be scary; a robber might come.

Bless the police and cats for their active role in the *chinuch* of our kids.

With our older kids, we sometimes use a more age appropriate and extremely potent proxy called *shidduchim*. It's something of a code word that's laden with meaning. We apply it freely when we want to get our child to toe the line:

They have to daven on time because of *shidduchim*.

They need to spend a few hours learning in shul during *bein hazmanim* because of *shidduchim*.

They have to improve their interpersonal skills because of *shidduchim*.

It's amazing how this word is so versatile that we each custom tailor it to cover all areas where our child could use improvement.

Now we know that these proxies really have absolutely nothing to do with *chinuch*! They have everything to do with our very own insecurities! Whenever we feel powerless against our children, out comes a proxy. We often blame our decisions — especially unpopular ones — on outside forces. That is using proxies. Yes, it helps make our parenting a little easier, but it's not real parenting. We're not teaching our kids anything.

When they're younger, we're depriving them of valuable lessons, such as listening to parents, not wandering off on their own, and road safety. When they're older, we're squandering many great opportunities to have quality conversations with our teens. When utilized appropriately, these opportunities could be used to help them gain an appreciation of the values we're trying to impart. It could help them gain a sense of self and responsibility. Instead, we're just cashing in on their fear instinct! Why should we willingly allow the police or the *shadchan* to deprive us of those *chinuch* opportunities?

Furthermore, the fear tactic is of limited value. At some point, our kids will call our bluff. The younger ones might come to realize that we won't actually make them sleep with the cats and the police won't come if they misbehave. Our older ones will become disgusted with their need to play pretend just because of our ominous fear of *shidduchim*. Once that happens, we have no leverage over them and we've taught them no true values. What a loss of time and resources!

Let's grab the opportunities when they present themselves! With some investment we can learn how to actually deal with the hardships and we could try to find real solutions to the issues. True, it calls for more effort on our part. Indeed, it calls for some real parenting skills! But it's a great investment!

Our children will learn that parental authority is indisputable. They'll learn that there are rules and possibly consequences for breaking those rules.

We will learn to build a solid and healthy relationship with our teens. They will have an opportunity to thrive in the atmosphere of mutual understanding and real dialogue. They'll be able to voice their doubts and concerns without any looming threats. We, in turn, will learn when to be firm and when to be lenient with our teens.

Most importantly, the *shadchanim* and police will now be free to do their work!

When we have a solid case, there is no need for a scary face!

CONCLUSION

When I showed this book to a close friend of mine, he asked me in wonder if I have actually mastered all the areas I wrote about. I told him that, to the contrary, I'm struggling in all these areas, and I can therefore identify with these inner struggles. As the Baal Shem Tov said, we can only see those shortcomings in others that we ourselves have.

This can be understood with the psychological principle that we see the world through our inner filters. Thus, if something shows up on our screen, it's proof that it's part of our program. All the issues that I wrote about obviously showed up on my screen. That's why I was able to really understand them.

Writing about them has afforded me an opportunity to dissect these issues and to seek solutions for them. When a problem in my life arose, I was sometimes struck with the recognition that I've written a solution for this very predicament. I had no choice but to try it. Thus, I myself was arguably the greatest beneficiary of my own advice.

Biased as I am, I can testify that they work. It's my fervent hope that the readers will also be courageous enough to try out some of the techniques and ideas mentioned. I am confident that it will have a great positive impact on your lives!

APPENDIX
Brief Biography of the Ohr HaChaim

Rabbi Chaim ben Moshe ibn Attar was born in 5456 (1696) in Sali, Morocco to a family that had produced many outstanding Torah scholars. He was named Chaim in honor of his paternal grandfather. Rabbi Chaim studied along with his cousins under the tutelage of their saintly grandfather, the senior Rabbi Chaim. They would begin their day at midnight when they mourned the Destruction, and then they would learn until daybreak followed by a full day of learning.

Rabbi Chaim married Patzonia, daughter of the great philanthropist R' Moshe from Meknes (his father's cousin). He was generously supported by his father-in-law and he continued to study Torah very diligently. Despite his young age, he taught Torah to the public. (He would eventually marry a second wife, Esther.) His wives were righteous in their own right and reportedly wore *tefillin*.

This period of calm in Rabbi Chaim's life didn't last long. At that time, Morocco was beset with political turmoil and infighting among the ruling family. As always, the Jews suffered the most. The community of Sali had to disperse and the Jews settled in different cities. Rabbi Moshe had close connections at court which he utilized to help his brethren. But in the end, he suffered terribly from the authorities and from people within the community.

After his father-in-law's passing, Rabbi Chaim inherited a large portion of his father-in-law's suffering. The authorities continued persecuting Rabbi Moshe's family. People who didn't dare to sue Rabbi Moshe himself in *beis din* for various perceived injustices, felt it convenient to do so to his heirs. Rabbi Chaim's life was even in danger on more than one occasion. He was much more pained from the harassment by his coreligionists than from the authorities.

Rabbi Chaim eventually returned to Sali where he opened a yeshiva that he funded himself. He learned most of the day and spent a minimal amount of time plying his trade as a silversmith. In Sali, he printed his first *sefer*, *Chefetz Hashem*. While he went about his holy work, his misery didn't abate.

When he'd suffered his fill, Rabbi Chaim decided to leave Morocco for good and settle in Eretz Yisrael. On his way to Eretz Yisrael, he passed the city of Fes, and Rabbi Shmuel Elbaz appointed him to head the yeshiva. After a few years of relative peace, a heavy famine struck Morocco which led to the almost complete devastation of Fes.

There was no point in staying in Fes, thus Rabbi Chaim continued his trek to Eretz Yisrael. He joined a caravan to traverse the vast desert. On the way, Rabbi Chaim experienced many great miracles. On the eve of their first Shabbos, Rabbi Chaim notified the rest of the caravan that he was not willing to travel on Shabbos. They told him that by no means would they spend an additional day in the dangerous desert just resting. Having no choice, he separated from the rest and settled down, with his family, in the wilderness. Right before Shabbos, a ferocious lion approached their small encampment and sat guard next to them for the duration of Shabbos. The rest of the caravan, having lost their way, found themselves after Shabbos back at the place where they had left Rabbi Chaim, and they witnessed the great miracle.[86]

---

86   *Shulchan Ha'Tahor, Hilchos Shabbos* 248.

After much travail, he finally reached the city of Livorno, Italy on the eve of Shavuos 5499. Rabbi Chaim decided to settle down in Livorno for a while. The community provided him comfortably with all his needs and it was there that with the help of the community he published his *sefarim, Ohr HaChaim* and *Pri To'ar*.

While in Italy, Rabbi Chaim worked diligently to gather a group of promising young scholars for his yeshiva. He also established a network of wealthy individuals who took it upon themselves to fully support his yeshiva in Yerushalayim. On Rosh Chodesh Av, he set sail from Livorno with a core group of ten disciples and their families. They reached the port of Acre in the end of Elul.

Due to an epidemic that was raging at that time in Yerushalayim, he settled for the time being in Acre and established his yeshiva there. It was only about a year later that the group headed out for Yerushalayim.

Once there, Rabbi Chaim established his yeshiva in the very court-yard where the holy Ari was born. According to Chassidic tradition, he actually established two *yeshivos*, one for studying the revealed Torah and one for studying the hidden parts of the Torah. The latter yeshiva was a secretive one and very few people were even aware of it. The Baal Shem Tov's brother-in-law, Rabbi Gershon of Kitov was among the few prized students of that yeshiva.

Alas, Rabbi Chaim wasn't destined to enjoy a peaceful life in the holy city. He passed away on Shabbos, 14th of Tammuz 5503, less than a year after his arrival. On that Shabbos, the Baal Shem Tov announced to his disciples, "The western candle has been extinguished."

Rabbi Chaim became known by the name of his *sefer, Ohr HaChaim*. He was forty-seven when he passed away. He was buried on the Mount of Olives. At his side were also buried his two wives.

The Ohr HaChaim's grave has been a drawing site for many people seeking salvation. In the summer of 1942, there was a terrible fear that the Nazi forces under the leadership of field marshal Erwin Rommel would conquer Eretz Yisrael. A massive prayer rally was organized at the grave of the Ohr HaChaim led by the venerated Chassidic *rebbes* Rabbi Yisrael of Husyatin and Rabbi Shlomo of Zvhil. After a while

Rabbi Yisrael told those gathered that "he won't come." And so it was. The very next day, the battle at El Alamein broke out. Against all odds, Rommel was defeated. The Jews in the Holy Land were safe.

Between 1948 and 1967, when East Jerusalem was under Jordanian rule, the Jordanians wanted to construct a road that would run through the Mount of Olives. They destroyed countless graves on the way. As soon as the bulldozer neared the grave of the Ohr HaChaim, it turned over and the driver was killed. The Jordanians tried a second time and a third time, but after three people died there they finally abandoned the project. In 1967, when Jews returned to the Mount of Olives, they discovered the half-cleared road cutting through the cemetery up to the Ohr HaChaim's grave just as it had been left.

While a great many years have passed since the passing of Rabbi Chaim, it's possible to get a glimpse of his greatness through his great work, *Ohr HaChaim*. Rabbi Moshe of Kubrin said that by learning the *Ohr HaChaim* one could reach a level as if he would be hearing the words directly from the mouth of Rabbi Chaim.[87]

---

87   Rabbi Moshe Chaim Kleinman, *Ohr Yesharim* 81.

GLOSSARY

Aseres Hadibros: the Ten Commandments.

askan (askanim – pl.): community activist(s).

askanus: the field of community activism.

avodah: lit., work; the ceremonial work in the Holy Temple performed by *kohanim*, the decedents of Aharon.

avodas Hashem: the service of G-d.

Avos: the biblical Patriarchs.

baal teshuvah: a person who repents, returns to Torah lifestyle.

baal simchah (baalei simchah – pl.): host(s) of a celebration.

Balak ben Tzipor: a Midyanite prince who became king of Moab.

bechirah: the ability to exercise free will.

bachur (bachurim – pl.): male(s) from age thirteen until marriage.

bein hazmanim: intersession break in *yeshivos*.

Beis El: the city of Bethel.

Beis Hamikdash: the Holy Temple in Jerusalem.

ben sorer u'moreh: a wayward son who doesn't listen to his parents, indulges in excess meat and wine, and steals.

Bilam: a biblical prophet of the gentiles.

blatt (Y.): a folio, a page in the Talmud.

Bnei Yisrael: the Hebrews, the Jewish nation.

chanayos: places of rest.

Chassidus: a branch of Orthodox Judaism, founded by Rabbi Yisroel Baal Shem Tov; the teachings, interpretations, and various practices of Judaism as articulated by the Chassidic movement; a Chassidic subgroup.

chavrusah (chavrusos – pl.) (A.): study partner(s).

Chazal: an acronym for *Chachameinu zichronam li-vrachah*; lit., our Sages, may their memory be blessed; the Sages of the Mishnah and Talmud.

cheder: lit., room; primary school for religious boys.

chillul Hashem: desecration of G-d's name.

chinuch: the transmission of the tenets, principles and religious laws of Judaism.

daven (davening): pray(ing).

dayan: a rabbinic judge.

eigel: the sin of the Golden Calf.

Eisav: Esau, Jacob's twin brother.

Emori: Emorites, an ancient people who occupied large tracts of Syria and northern Israel.

Eretz Yisrael: Land of Israel.

frum (Y.): religiously observant; devout.

Gan Eden: Garden of Eden, heaven, paradise.

Gedolei Yisrael: great Torah leaders.

Gehinnom: purgatory.

gemach: an acronym for *gemilas chasadim* (lit., doing kindness); a free loan fund.

Gemara: the Babylonian Talmud.

gilgul: reincarnation.

halachah: Jewish law.

hekdesh: property of the Holy Temple; property of a synagogue or religious educational institution.

hishtadlus: the effort one invests in obtaining/reaching a given objective/goal.

Ish ha'Elokim: G-dly man.

kedushah: sanctity, holiness.

kehillah: a congregation.

ketores: an incense offering in the Holy Temple.

kiddush: sanctification of the Sabbath and festivals, usually recited over a cup of wine.

kiddush Hashem: sanctification of G-d's Name.

klal: the general populace.

Klal Yisrael: the Jewish nation.

kollel: a center for advanced Torah study for adult students, mostly married men.

kohanim: members of the priestly tribe; descendants of Aharon.

korban (korbanos – pl.): sacrificial offering(s) at the Holy Temple.

korban Pesach: the Passover sacrificial offering that was slaughtered on Passover eve and eaten in the evening.

krias Shema: the recital of the three Torah portions commencing with *Shema Yisrael,* Deuteronomy 6:4–9, 11:13–21, and Numbers 15:37–41.

Lavan: Laban, father of the biblical Matriarchs Rachel and Leah.

Ma'adim: the planet Mars.

Maariv: the evening prayer service.

mabul: lit., a flood; the great flood in the times of Noah.

Magen David: lit., the Shield of David; Protector of David.

maggid: lit., a preacher; oftentimes referring to a Chassidic religious leader.

Markulis: an idol that was worshipped through throwing stones at it.

masa'os: travels.

mashgiach: one in charge of students' moral well-being in a yeshiva.

masmid: a diligent student.

matzah: unleavened bread eaten during the festival of Passover.

mazal (mazalos – pl.): constellation(s); planet(s); destiny.

mechanech: a pedagogue; to educate.

mechutanim: the parents of one's son-in-law or daughter-in-law.

mei merivah: lit., the water of argument; the sin of Moses for hitting the rock instead of speaking to it in order to extract water.

meraglim: spies; scouts.

meshulach: a fundraiser; a person collecting money.

mesorah: Jewish tradition; the transmission of Jewish laws and tradition.

midbar: the desert.

middah (middos – pl.): character trait(s).

Midrash: early rabbinic compendium of legal or narrative material.

milah: circumcision.

Minchah: the afternoon prayer services.

Mishkan: the Tabernacle erected by the Jews in the desert.

Mishneh l'Melech: commentary on the Mishneh Torah of the Rambam.

Mitzvah (mitzvos – pl.): commandment(s).

Mitzrayim: Egypt.

mizbei'ach: an altar.

Moav: the ancient kingdom of Moab who lived in modern-day Jordan.

mohel: one who performs circumcisions.

mosdos: institutions.

nachas: pleasure, pride at seeing one's progeny succeeding.

nasi (nesi'im – pl.): an appointed tribal prince(s).

nazir (nezzirim – pl.): a nazirite(s).

nevuah: a prophecy.

nezirus: the act of being a nazirite.

nisayon (nisyonos – pl.): lit., a test; a challenge to foster spiritual growth.

Olam Habah: the World to Come.

ovdei Hashem: servants of G-d.

parnassah: livelihood.

patur: one dismissed from legal accountability.

Pe'or: an idol that was worshipped through relieving oneself in its presence.

Pesach: Passover.

pasuk: a verse from Scriptures.

peirush: an elucidation; a commentary on a given text.

perek: a chapter.

Raavad: Rabbi Avraham ben David (1120–1198). He was among the early kabbalists and an eminent commentator on the Talmud. He was one of the foremost critics of the Rambam and his comments were printed alongside the text of the Rambam's work, *Mishneh Torah.*

Rambam: Rabbi Moshe ben Maimon, aka Maimonides (1134–1204). He was one of the most well-known Torah authorities of all time. His magnum opus was *Mishneh Torah* in which he codified the entire body of Jewish law.

rav (rabbanim – pl.): rabbi(s).

Rashi: Rabbi Shlomo Yitzchaki (1040–1104) was a highly esteemed medieval French rabbi and author of a comprehensive commentary on the Talmud and the *Tanach.* Acclaimed for his ability to present the basic meaning of the text in a concise and lucid fashion, Rashi appeals to both learned scholars and beginning students.

rebbi (Y.): a Torah teacher.

rosh yeshiva: the dean of a yeshiva.

seder: a learning session.

sefer (sefarim – pl.): book(s).

shadchan: a matchmaker.

shamayim: lit., the sky; heaven.

Shechem: the city of Nablus.

sheva brachos: the seven blessings recited at a wedding; celebrations held during the week following a wedding.

shidduch (shidduchim – pl.): marital match(es).

shochet: a slaughterer of kosher meat.

shogeg: an unintentional sin; an unintentional sinner.

shul: a synagogue.

shvigger (Y.): a mother-in-law.

simchah: joy; celebration.

sinas chinam: baseless hatred.

sneh: thorn bush; the thorn bush where G-d first revealed himself to Moses.

succah: a temporary hut constructed for use during the week-long Jewish festival of Sukkot and topped with branches.

Succos: Sukkot.

talmid chacham: a Torah scholar.

Tana'im: the Sages who compiled the Mishnah.

teshuvah: repentance, return to Torah lifestyle.

Toras Chaim: Torah of Life.

Toras Emes: Torah of Truth.

Tzaddik (tzaddikim – pl.): a righteous man/men.

Yarden: the Jordan River.

Yerushalayim: the city of Jerusalem.

yeshiva: an academy of Torah study.

yetzer hara: the evil inclination.

Yid/Yidden (Y.): Jew(s).

Yiddishkeit (Y.): Judaism.

Yisro: Jethro, father-in-law of Moses.

Rabbi Langsam has accomplished a formidable task in this beautiful work. He has combined timeless Torah lessons with psychological principles and insights. While this is a monumental feat in its own right, Rabbi Langsam has fused these two worlds in a highly accessible and user friendly manner. This book — with its inspiring and illuminating style that lifts the soul — will be a welcome addition in any Torah home that values the time-honored traditions of *tikkun hamiddos* and *cheshbon hanefesh*. In today's ever growing world of disconnect, the lessons learned here will facilitate an added desire and commitment to slow life down just enough to actually enjoy it!

Ashrecha and *yeyasher kochacha*!
GAVRIEL FAGIN, PHD